Cheating[*]

An Inside Look at the Bad Things Good NASCAR Winston Cup Racers Do in Pursuit of Speed

BY TOM JENSEN

DAVID BULL PUBLISHING

Library of Congress Cataloging-in-Publication Data is available.

ISBN: 1 893618 22 6

David Bull Publishing, logo, and colophon are trademarks of David Bull Publishing, Inc.

Book and cover design: Tom Morgan, Blue Design, Portland, Maine

Printed in the United States

10 9 8 7 6 5 4 3 2 1

David Bull Publishing
4250 East Camelback Road
Suite K150
Phoenix, AZ 85018

602-852-9500
602-852-9503 (fax)

www.bullpublishing.com

Page 2- *A NASCAR inspector examines a restrictor plate prior to its installation. Because restrictor plates cut horsepower in half, crew chiefs and engineers have constantly tried to figure out ways to work around them. (Tom Copeland)*
Page 6- *NASCAR is so secretive about its regulations that it does not even make its rulebook available to the general public and alters it whenever it sees fit. (Tom Copeland)*
Page 8- *The so-called "long template" literally runs nose-to-tail on a Winston Cup car, as witnessed in this shot of Jerry Nadeau's Chevrolet at Watkins Glen in 2001. (Sam Sharpe)*

Table of Contents

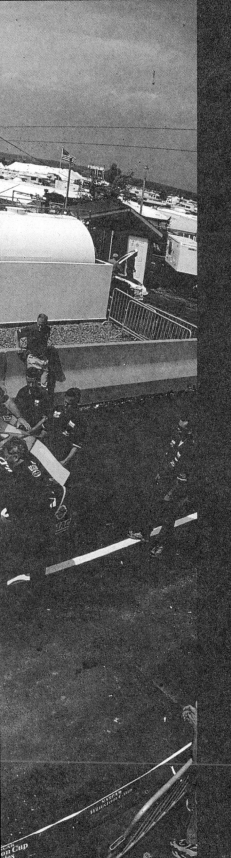

Introduction

Someone always will figure out how to get around the rules, even though we try to make them as clear as possible. Lawyers and accountants have been doing that with the tax code for years.

—NASCAR chairman Bill France Jr.

Introduction
All in the Family

In auto racing as in life, cheating happens. It always has and it always will. Bad guys do it, but so do nice guys. Within the closely knit community of NASCAR stock-car racers, cheating is an acknowledged part of the sport, though one that is rarely discussed in the polite company of outsiders, especially for the record. In private, some racers will brag about cheating with the cocky bravado and explicit detail of a frat boy who just bedded the head cheerleader. But in the cold light of day, and with cameras and tape recorders rolling, some of these same men tap dance around the subject and parse words in ways that would make Bill Clinton look like a piker. After more than half a century of stock-car racing, it's time to set the record straight, or as straight as it can be, anyway, on one of the sport's most storied and colorful traditions.

When David Bull and I stood outside of the Atlanta Motor Speedway infield media center in November 1999 and agreed to produce a book about the history of cheating in NASCAR, it seemed like a fairly straightforward proposition. Although no one had ever put together a comprehensive chronicle of cheating over the course of the sport's history, many individual episodes have become part of stock-car racing folklore.

There was everything from Junior Johnson's infamous "Yellow Banana," a radically reshaped 1966 Ford Galaxie, to Smokey Yunick allegedly driving away from tech inspection at Daytona a year later without the benefit of a gas tank. There was Mark Martin and Jack Roush losing the 1990 Winston Cup championship over an intake manifold spacer that had been bolted rather than welded in place. There were "bootlegger springs," "soaked" tires, nitrous oxide, and "Tiregate." It seemed like it wouldn't be too complicated to connect the dots, so to speak, from the first NASCAR "Strictly Stock" series race in 1949 until the 2001 season.

As it turned out, connecting the dots wasn't especially difficult, though finding the definitive, irrefutable truth was. More than 80 people were interviewed for this book, most by myself during the last 18 months of my four-year tenure as executive editor of *NASCAR Winston Cup Scene,* and about 15 more by Mike Hembree, a veteran journalist who has been covering the Winston Cup beat for more than two decades.

We talked to drivers, crew chiefs, mechanics, car owners, NASCAR officials, track workers, and other journalists, people who are active in the sport today and those long since retired. Two of our subjects, Smokey Yunick and Jack Smith, gave their final interviews on the subject of cheating before they died. We heard tales of all the major areas one can cheat on a race car: engine, fuel capacity, weight, aerodynamics, handling, and tires. Most of the reporting of events over the last five years took place at racetracks, as incidents happened that we personally witnessed.

We heard a lot of interesting stories, some contradictory, others surely embellished. I'm not naive enough to believe everyone told us the truth, the whole truth, and nothing but the truth. Clearly, some of the information dispensed was self-serving and designed to misdirect. And in some cases, memories of events that happened 40 or 50 years ago might be hazy at best. Still, taken in their entirety, some startling stories about the sport and the men in it emerged. In compiling this research and doing the interviews, I was reminded of the words of Big Chief in the brilliant opening of Ken Kesey's *One Flew over the Cuckoo's Nest:* "But it's the truth, even if it never happened."

And at Daytona and Darlington, as in Hollywood, there aren't any truly new story lines. Racers are trying to do today what they tried 10, 20, or 50 years ago: Get more power under the hood, more traction from the tires and chassis, more gas in the car, and better aerodynamics—then publicly deny they've done any of the above.

While cheating is a great subject to talk about over a few beers on Saturday night, men who make their living in racing are no more eager to go on the record about cheating in the garage than they would be to go on the record about cheating on their wives, another popular but not publicly discussed pastime among some in the sport. In the business of racing, you don't crap where you eat, especially not in NASCAR, which since its inception in 1947 has been run as an only-sometimes-benevolent dictatorship, first by Big Bill France and then by his son, Bill Jr.

Grudges get held for a long time here, and reputations are soiled easily, which is why few in the sport will openly admit that they cheat or have ever cheated. They don't want a slip of the tongue to incur the wrath and subsequent retaliation of NASCAR or, worse yet, end up costing them a lucrative corporate sponsorship. Cheating is a four-letter word for NASCAR and sponsors alike. Nobody likes to be called a cheater in public and no one likes their name associated with cheating scandals, so people weren't exactly lining up on my doorstep with their true confessions.

Still, they 'fessed up more than I thought they might at first, though in some very specific ways. While researching this book, a couple of common themes emerged. First and foremost, to a man, everyone interviewed swore there was more cheating five years ago or 20 years ago or 50 years ago or two weeks ago than there is today. "I think in the 1960s, '70s and '80s probably every race that was won was won with something that wasn't quite right," said former crew chief Larry McReynolds, echoing an oft-heard sentiment. "Today almost every race that is won is won with straight stuff."

Second, most everyone interviewed swore the other guys did a lot more cheating than they did. It's human nature, I suppose.

I even heard a suggestion that people would be a lot more forthcoming if we could somehow use a word other than "cheating" to describe what they and others had been doing over the last half century.

"We should have invented another name for cheating," said Lowe's Motor Speedway President H. A. "Humpy" Wheeler. "That's the thing that's gotten us some bad ink. Cheating, I guess Webster would define it as an infringement of the rules. If we could come up with another name for it, it probably wouldn't be so bad. The negative part of it is not to the people who follow the sport. They understand it and laugh about it, particularly when somebody gets caught red-handed. It's a little bit like drinking. It's funny when somebody does something when they've had a little bit too much. It's not funny when somebody hits somebody else head-on and kills people. The same thing with cheating."

Even the most flagrant scofflaws served up some brilliant rationalizations for why what they did wasn't really cheating. "I tried to stay away from any cheating thing that was against the rules," claimed Junior Johnson, a man whose considerable talents will be detailed later. "I went outside the rule book and worked all the time."

While racers are loath to come flat out and say they actively cheated, there isn't a crew chief, mechanic, car owner or driver in today's Winston Cup garage who won't tell you he's "pushed the envelope" or "rode it to the edge" or sought a "competitive advantage" or "looked for the gray areas" in the rule book. And they'll insist it's no worse than in any other form of racing.

"I think you have the same thing in Formula One and you have the same thing in Champ cars, Indy cars, drag racing," car owner Richard Childress told me. "I think it's competitiveness. We've always used the term 'trying to get a competitive edge' instead of cheating. I don't like the word 'cheating.' It's trying to get a competitive edge on your competitors."

"We call it self-defense, not cheating," added Barry Dodson, who was Rusty Wallace's crew chief during his championship run in 1989.

There is an implicit code among racers: It's not cheating unless you get caught, and even then it's something to be laughed off privately no matter how much public outrage one has to feign to make it look good to the media or other outsiders.

I stood in the garage at New Hampshire International Speedway in 1999 interviewing Ray Evernham, Jeff Gordon's crew chief, when Tony Glover from Team Sabco began to walk by. All of a sudden, Evernham's voice grew loud and animated: "Like I was saying, you'd have to be a real dumbass to try something like what Sabco did at Daytona last week," he said, speaking with far too much volume for Glover to ignore. Instead, Glover walked over, Evernham threw his arm around him, and they both had a good laugh about the illegal and carefully disguised intake manifold insert Sabco had been caught with during the Pepsi 400 at Daytona—and fined $50,000 for.

NASCAR was outraged, and publicly the other teams were shocked to find cheating going on at Daytona. But privately, racers will tell you it's part of the game.

Whether you call it cheating or looking for a competitive edge, the list of who's run afoul of NASCAR covers most every big-name stock racer of all time: Richard Petty got caught with an oversized engine, Darrell Waltrip with a canister of nitrous oxide, Jeff Gordon with titanium hubs. Before he became a captain of industry, car owner Roger Penske's team motto was "The unfair advantage."

On the other hand, to be completely fair to the racers, a lot of guys over the years won races with cars that were 100 percent legal at the time they ran, only to have NASCAR later change the rules when it discovered how those cars had gained an advantage. Racers, and crew chiefs, in particular, spend an inordinate amount of time trying to think outside the box in an effort to improve performance. It's just that their box is the NASCAR rule book. It's always been that way.

When Richard Petty won 27 races in 1967, including a record 10 in a row, his car was vastly superior to the competition because his team figured out before anyone else did that a stock car would handle better by putting as much weight on the driver's side as possible, which made turning into corners easier. When NASCAR finally figured out what Petty was doing, it mandated weight distribution for each side of the car and Petty lost his advantage. No one, least of all me, would suggest that Petty's record should in any way carry a taint.

By the same token, in 1991, Harry Gant won four races in a row and nearly took a fifth before his brakes failed late in the race at North Wilkesboro. Gant's sudden performance gain occurred because his crew chief Andy Petree had the idea of a cambered rear axle, one that tilted the rear wheels almost imperceptibly to the left, another modification designed to make the car turn easier, which it did. NASCAR found out about it, probably on a tip from another team, discreetly changed its rules to bar such a fix, and Gant suddenly went from being unstoppable to mediocre again. Nobody accused his team of cheating.

"A lot of things people have done over the years have caused NASCAR to rewrite the rule book," said Larry McReynolds, now a Fox TV commentator. "It maybe was not an infraction when they did it, but it didn't take long for them to make a rule regarding it."

It's a racer's job to innovate; it's NASCAR's job to police the racers. NASCAR managing director of competition Gary Nelson, himself a master of circumventing the rule book before moving from the crew chief ranks to become NASCAR's top policeman at the end of 1991, explained it this way. "Racers race 24 hours a day. That's all they do," he told me in an interview in Richmond during the 2000 season. "All they think about and everything they do is directed toward beating the other guy. If somebody talks to you it's because he's racing you. He wants to get the advantage on you."

Nelson, of course, is absolutely right. Every race day, 43 guys try to go out and outrun and outwit each other. Competition is as much a part of their genetic makeup as hair color. And in the intense pressure-packed crucible of Winston Cup, where sponsorships are worth many millions of dollars a year and race crowds top 200,000 people on a Sunday afternoon, the weight of expectations can be crushing.

"Would I pay $50,000 for a win or for a tenth [of a second]? In a heartbeat," driver/owner Kyle Petty said. "Every Winston Cup driver and every Winston Cup owner out here would. These [sponsors] are paying you millions of dollars to run up front, not run at the back, so you use everything you can. It's very tempting for a lot of people."

The temptation has always been there, but the economic changes in the sport upped the ante dramatically. As the 1990s began, teams could run a full season for about $1 million; by the end of the decade, annual budgets were 10 to 20 times that for top teams.

By 2000, Winston Cup primary sponsors were paying anywhere from $5 million to $15 million a year to have their names and logos splashed across brightly colored race cars and probably twice that to "activate their sponsorships," a marketing euphemism that refers to the endless collateral promotional activities sponsors engage in. Whether it was Budweiser producing 10,000 life-size cardboard cutouts of Dale Earnhardt Jr. to place in front of beer displays at convenience stores from Key West to Seattle, or DuPont entertaining 1,000 body-shop owners trackside, sponsorship has become a huge growth industry. And the closer a sponsor's car runs to the front, the happier that sponsor is.

Above everything else—the marketing benefits, product sales, hospitality events and luxury suites—attracting four dozen companies to pay the millions of dollars it takes to play in Winston Cup cars requires one thing of NASCAR: "It's extremely important that every competitor and every sponsor feels like they have an equal chance to win, whether it's Jeff Gordon or the guy who qualifies 43rd," said Mike Helton, then NASCAR's senior vice president and chief operating officer.

To ensure a level playing field and keep sponsors coming to the track, Helton and NASCAR Winston Cup director Gary

Nelson have buttoned down the inspection process considerably over the past five years. NASCAR has made it a priority to significantly improve the level of training of its inspectors and hire more and better inspectors in the first place.

But it's an uphill struggle; when a talented young man with a penchant for things mechanical wants to get into stock-car racing, he has a choice. He can go to work for NASCAR and earn maybe $50,000 to $75,000 a year as an inspector, or go to work for a race team and make $150,000 to $300,000 as a top mechanic or engineer, and maybe, eventually, $1 million or more as a crew chief. For many, the choice is easy. Most of the inspectors are older men who are in it to be in the game, to be part of the sport. Most of the younger guys, while they love racing, are in it for themselves. The pay disparity is nothing new, nor is the balance of top-tier talent, which clearly favors the teams.

At every race, the cars line up end to end and go through as many as six inspections from prior to practice to post-race teardown. As part of the ritual every weekend, crew members surround each car in the inspection line, in part because they have to push the cars by hand through the line, in part to keep fans and members of other crews away.

Against the backdrop of a garage area crowded with 5,000 to 10,000 people, teams guard their cars closely, lest some yahoo wants to touch their car, or worse. You'll also see crew guys walk over to other cars in the inspection line, ostensibly to b.s. with their buddies, but really to check out the competition, to see how another team might have ever-so-subtly altered a fender flare or roofline in a way undetectable to the average eye, but easily discerned by someone who's spent the last 20 or 30 years in racing. Depending on how that buddy's car is running, the other team just might try it themselves later.

Once the cars reach the garage, it becomes the job of NASCAR's inspectors to police them. There are 60 or so inspectors who use up to 30 body templates per car to make sure the exterior dimensions conform to measurements that in some cases are as little as forty one-thousandths of an inch. Engine displacements and compression ratios are similarly tightly controlled. The weight of the car at all four corners is measured with sophisticated electronic scales. Fuel samples are taken from every car, some more than once, and the cars are required to maintain a minimum roof height and ground clearance. Everything that can be checked on the car, from tires to roof flaps, is checked, usually multiple times.

During the course of a weekend, the cars will be checked for integrity of safety items; for engine size and compression ratio; legality of all components, which must be specifically approved by NASCAR for use in the race; for precise body shape and contour. In an effort to equalize competition and cut down on cheating at some tracks, shock absorbers, rear springs, and carburetor restrictor plates are handed out at random prior to cars taking the track each time.

All of this is done to make sure every car complies with the NASCAR Winston Cup rule book—a publication that NASCAR does not even make available to the general public because it prefers to operate behind closed doors and to open up the rule book to outsiders would invite criticism and public second guessing, something NASCAR is sensitive to. The rule book is also a constantly evolving document, subject to change any time NASCAR feels it needs to take away an obvious advantage from one team or brand of car, to "level the playing field." And that furtive nature, the code of secrecy and silence, only fuels the atmosphere of paranoia and conspiracy in the garage.

Still, I am absolutely convinced after researching this project that NASCAR does do the most it can to eliminate cheating. As you'll read in subsequent chapters, the window of opportunity for rules violations has grown progressively smaller, especially in the last decade. People still try to cheat, but I think NASCAR is doing a better job of catching them than ever before.

As the sport's popularity exploded in the early 1990s, NASCAR hired Nelson, one of the most creative thinkers on the job, to police the cheating, a move most applauded. McReynolds put it rather succinctly: "If you've got a 7-Eleven that's been held up a dozen times and you can't catch that crook, maybe the best thing you could do is go hire a crook that's held up a 7-Eleven a lot. I'm not saying Gary is a crook. He was a very innovative thinker. He always was trying to figure out ways to get around the rules, to work hard in the gray area. And he always did a pretty good job at it."

As you'll read later on, Nelson is the one man who receives nearly universal praise for cleaning up the sport and clamping down on rampant cheating. Dimensions that used to be eyeballed in the 1980s are measured precisely and consistently now, which has forced teams to conform much more closely to the rules, and has satisfied them that the game is fair for all competitors today.

Yes, cheating still goes on. But there's a whole lot more to it than that, and the word "cheating" is a gross oversimplification of an act that is part cultural, part political, and part competitive.

As Dick Thompson, the longtime PR director at Martinsville Speedway and one of the most respected men in the sport put it, "They say you can interpret the rule book about like the Bible." Make no mistake about it either, crew chiefs and inspectors argue over the nuances of the NASCAR rule book with the same zeal and tenacity as religious leaders do scripture. This is serious stuff, and has been from the get-go.

As I delved deeper into this project, I realized that the behind-the-scenes psychology and politics of cheating were as interesting and complicated as the specific instances themselves. Often what happened wasn't nearly as fascinating as why it happened and how it happened and the repercussions that came out of it.

All of which is a way of setting the stage and saying that this book isn't as much an encyclopedia of cheating as a celebration of the creativity of racers and the tenacity of those who police them. It is meant to educate the reader, not impugn the characters of those in racing, even the most flagrant rule benders.

I truly hope you enjoy this book, have fun and learn something about the sport, too. And most of all, I hope it makes you think. I've deliberately tried to stick with telling the story and stay away from moralizing or preaching. As Nelson told me at Daytona in February 2001, "What we have is what we have. We're not trying to gloss over anything."

Tom Jensen
March 15, 2002

ALL IN THE FAMILY

NASCAR founder William Henry Getty France, better known as "Big Bill," organized stock-car racing and in the process used brains, will, and muscle to mostly tame a group of bootleggers and fringe-element racers. (Ken Breslauer collection)

Chapter 1

If you really look at it, in the first race, they disqualified the first winner. It started right off the bat. Someone had an idea: "Hey, I can get an edge with this." That still continues today.

—Dick Thompson

Original Sins

Wilham Henry Getty France had plenty of reasons to smile on the morning of June 19, 1949. His fledgling National Association for Stock Car Automobile Racing was about to host the very first race in its new "Strictly Stock" series, which France predicted would capture the imagination of race fans hungry for action in post–World War II America.

The first NASCAR Strictly Stock race was a key victory for the former Washington, D.C., gas station mechanic that everyone in the loose-knit racing fraternity knew as "Big Bill." The crowd gathered at the dusty three-quarter-mile Charlotte Speedway proved beyond a doubt that fans were interested in watching honest-to-God stock cars race: Hudsons and Kaisers and Lincolns and Fords that regular folks drove, not the fancy open-wheelers at Indianapolis or the bastardized "Modifieds" that looked like they'd been wrecked and rebuilt even before the race started.

And the cars literally were stock cars. There were no tube frames or aerodynamic sheet metal, no exotic racing fuel or slick, high-grip tires. The cars raced at Charlotte were vehicles that drivers had purchased at their local Lincoln or Ford or Hudson dealership and raced as they were, with only the most rudimentary safety modifications. Unlike today, when race cars are rolling sponsor billboards, the first Strictly Stock cars carried crude, hand-painted numbers and the driver's name and little else. In the few rare cases where cars had sponsors, the sponsor was usually a gas station or a car dealership in the driver's hometown. There were no uniforms or million-dollar transporters back then, either. For the most part, drivers wore T-shirts and blue jeans and were regular guys out to have some fun on a Sunday afternoon.

"When they said Strictly Stock, that wasn't just the name of the division, that was the rule as well," said historian Bob Latford, who began working at stock-car races in 1946 and later served as public relations director for Charlotte and Atlanta Motor Speedways. "The only thing you could do was beef up the right-front hub, because all the tracks were dirt then and the wheels took a lot of abuse, bouncing around. The tracks were not well manicured. The wheels, right fronts especially, were subject to breaking. And they let 'em do a little there. That was all you could do. Engines had to be essentially stock. Most of the cars still had their headlights in 'em. They taped over those. Driver's doors, they took a leather belt, a dog collar, something like that, and strapped the door shut. For seat belts, some of 'em just used a piece of rope to tie themselves in." Strictly stock it was.

And that was precisely what the fans wanted to see, as witnessed by the Charlotte turnout. The number of people attending that first Strictly Stock race, like much of NASCAR's history, is shrouded in controversy and myth. The announced attendance was 23,000, though some estimates placed it as low as 13,000 people. Still, attracting even 13,000 people was a huge triumph, especially at a time when racing was in its infancy and Charlotte was smack in the middle of nowhere.

Just as important to France, the first Strictly Stock race was proof that he had established a leadership position in the war for the heart and soul of racing in the Southeast. Now he was ready to turn his attention to promoting the battles on the track.

For most of the 1930s and 1940s, automobile racing had been chaotic and disorganized at best and outright criminal at worst. Dozens of sanctioning bodies had come and gone, each of which seemed to carry some tortured-sounding acronym like USCRA or NARL or, worst of all, SCARS.

In fact, one of France's earliest rivals was O. Bruton Smith, who grew up poor in rural North Carolina but would go on to form an empire of automobile dealerships and then a host of racetracks. Smith's National Stock Car Racing Association, or NSCRA, was one of France's competitors, though not for long.

The many acronym-bearing sanctioning bodies were just as confusing to race fans then as the plethora of dot-coms in the late 1990s .... Nobody knew who the real stars were, nor what constituted a true championship series or a national champion driver. France knew that by organizing the racing community, he could end the confusion and put his rivals out of business. That's why he convened a meeting of 22 men on

December 14, 1947, in the Ebony Room of the Streamline Motel in Daytona Beach, Florida.

The men, described in a 1998 interview by attendee Sam Packard as a mixture of "Yankees, Southerners, and boot-leggers," sought to organize and better the sport for the interests of all involved. Promoters would be held accountable for race purses, and NASCAR would come up with rules for competitors and enforce them.

"We are all interested in one thing," France told the group. "That is improving present conditions. The answer lies in our group here today to do it." And so they did. Legendary mechanic Red Vogt was credited with coming up with NASCAR as the group's name, and well-known racer E. G. "Cannonball" Baker was named the first commissioner. Big Bill France, however, was the real center of power for the organization. It would need it.

Shady dealings were commonplace in racing. Local race promoters often would fail to deliver on promised prize money to the drivers. It was not unusual to see post-race events end in fisticuffs or much worse.

And many of the drivers weren't any better. While today cities like Charlotte and Atlanta and regions like Upstate South Carolina are testaments to the economic prosperity and boom times that Sun Belt chambers of commerce love to tout, half a century ago the Southeastern United States was still try-ing to recover from the ruinous effects of losing the Civil War. Put bluntly, the Southeast at that time was dirt poor in most places. Economic options were few: farming, usually tobacco or cotton, or working in the mills for little more than a subsistence wage.

Of course, there was one other option, and many of the South's best and brightest pursued it with ferocious abandon: moonshining. A lot more money was to be made selling corn liquor cooked in a backyard still than there was toiling away trying to raise crops or busting your ass in the mills.

Not that bottling and selling moonshine was without its hazards, mind you. Federal agents from what is now known as the Bureau of Alcohol, Tobacco and Firearms hunted for the stills and the men and women who ran them. Getting caught meant going to jail and going to jail meant your family had no source of income.

Out of necessity, moonshine runners learned to hop up their cars and drive them on the ragged edge. Their livelihood—indeed their very survival—depended on their ability to outwit and outdrive the dreaded federal agents known as "revenuers."

"It was a game of honor," said Latford. "Most of the revenuers knew who the bootleggers were. It was a matter of pride to try and catch 'em. And an equal matter of pride to try and outrun 'em. And a lot of it was argument between bootleggers: 'My hauler will outrun your hauler.' And they'd get together and get a grader or a bulldozer or tractor to cut out a little circle in a corn field or a tobacco field or a cotton field and go out there on weekends and race and bet with each other, sometimes for pretty good money."

The smartest of the 'shine runners would take tame, stock-appearing Ford coupes and replace the underpowered "flathead" motors under the hood with high-compression, overhead-valve Cadillac engines, the most powerful of the day. Then they would beef up the chassis with stiff springs so that it wouldn't sag under the load of a couple hundred gallons of corn liquor. "You didn't want to draw attention to it going down the road, but you wanted the ability to get away if they came after you," Latford said. "And you have to remember, they were running a lot heavier because of the liquid they were carrying than the pursuers were."

What the moonshine runners wanted was a car that looked completely stock to the untrained eye, but was the fastest car in the state in the wee hours of the morning. And what the feds lived for was catching these guys and running them down. It was exactly the kind of war of minds that crew chiefs and NASCAR inspectors would play out again and again in later eras.

And the moonshine runners were very, very good at what they did. Brothers Tim, Bob, and Fontello "Fonty" Flock from North Georgia were three well-known whiskey haulers of the late 1940s. And a guy from Wilkes County, North Carolina, named Junior Johnson would later make a name for himself, too.

France knew all about the whiskey running and the tricked-up cars and the wild men who drove them. And he set about organizing and controlling them. While NASCAR would sanction 52 races in 1948, its first full year in operation, the Strictly Stock division, which would eventually evolve into the Winston Cup Series over the next quarter-century, wouldn't get its start until Charlotte in June 1949. But when it did, it launched with a bang.

"Stock-car racing has boomed beyond anyone's wildest dreams, and I feel that we are in for another big year," France said in 1948. But even Big Bill didn't know how big. The first Strictly Stock race in Charlotte would give him a pretty good indication. And it would also give NASCAR its first controversy and the first of many unsuccessful challenges to France's authority.

•   •   •

In truth, nobody knew exactly what to expect at the first Strictly Stock race, and it showed. Parking and traffic were nightmares, just as they typically are at modern-day Winston Cup races. The concession stands sold out of food and drink.

"There were fans here at 6 a.m. that day," said David Allison, the son of track owner Carl Allison, in a 1998 interview with *NASCAR Winston Cup Scene* correspondent Mike Hembree. "People were trying to get in everywhere. We had people climbing trees to see. Daddy would crank up a chain saw and go over there. He wouldn't actually cut the trees down, but they would come out of them anyway. They never dreamed that many people would come to the first race." But they did, for one reason: They wanted to see their local heroes race stock cars, the very same kinds they drove.

And of course, the whole point of France's Strictly Stock series was just as the name implies: Cars were to be raced exactly as they had come off the showroom floor. The only exception was that racers were allowed to put a steel plate between the front wheels and brake drums to keep the wheels from stripping their studs and lug nuts and coming off the cars. That was it. Everything else had to be stock.

And that's how most of them raced on that hot, dusty day in Charlotte. There was Lee Petty from up near Greensboro in the northern part of the state, who had come down in an enormous and brand-new Buick Roadmaster sedan, which he would roll over and destroy in the race.

Buck Baker drove a Kaiser at Charlotte, and Bob Flock raced in a Hudson, while brother Tim somehow managed to borrow a brand-new Oldsmobile 88 with less than 1,000 miles on it from newlyweds Buddy and Betty Elliott of Hickory, North Carolina.

At the end of 200 laps, there was a lot of torn up machinery and dashed hopes. Crossing the finish line first was Glenn Dunnaway of Gastonia, North Carolina, about 25 miles southwest of Charlotte. Dunnaway, who had come to the race without a car to compete in, had hooked up with bootlegger Hubert Westmoreland, who installed him behind the wheel of his 1947 Ford coupe. His margin of victory was three laps.

But before Dunnaway could claim the $2,000 first-prize check, a small fortune in those days, NASCAR chief technical inspector Al Crisler disqualified him for having illegal "bootlegger springs" on the rear of the Westmoreland-owned Ford. The heavy-duty leaf springs helped distribute the weight better, which in turn improved handling. "They basically flip-flopped the springs and beefed up the rear end of the car. It was an old bootlegger trick, of course," said Latford. "A lot of the guys building the cars had built a lot of bootlegger cars."

Not everyone felt that Dunnaway should have been disqualified. "I think that was the worst injustice that I ever saw
NASCAR do anybody," veteran racer Jack Smith said in his
final interview, given just weeks before he died of heart failure at age 65 in October 2001. "The night before the race they
had tripped that car with whiskey on it. It had two pieces
welded on the back of the frame so the axle would go down
to there [limiting suspension travel and how low the car would
drop with a load of moonshine]. If anything, it would have
had to hurt him." But Crisler deemed it illegal, and Big Bill
France agreed.

Dunnaway's disqualification turned the race win over to Jim
Roper, who had driven nonstop all the way from Halstead,
Kansas, a distance of more than 1,000 miles, in a 1948
Lincoln. He had seen the race promoted in the syndicated
comic strip "Smilin' Jack."

Roper's engine was torn down in post-race inspection, and
he had to get a replacement motor from nearby Mecklenburg
Motors in order to drive the race-winning car back to Kansas.

Westmoreland, meanwhile, was incensed. He filed suit
against NASCAR in Mecklenburg County Court, in North
Carolina, asking for $5,000 in damages and saying he and
Dunnaway were unfairly robbed of the victory. But the suit was
subsequently thrown out and actually worked to France's
advantage, because as Latford put it, a court of law decided
"that he [France] could make and administer the rules for the
organization." This was a crucial victory, given the fledgling
nature of the sanctioning body and the outlaw mindset of many
of its participants.

The scenario would be repeated often over NASCAR's illustrious history: A huge crowd witnessed a race steeped in
controversy that would be talked about for days to come. A
competitor would be caught cheating and be punished, and
NASCAR's authority would be challenged, unsuccessfully. It's
a theme that would be repeated over and over again as stock-
car racing grew. Such twists and turns and rumors and
innuendo would help fuel the growth of the sport over the next
half century and beyond.

"If you really look at it, in the first race, they disqualified
the first winner," said Dick Thompson, the longtime public relations director for Martinsville Speedway. "It started right off
the bat. Someone had an idea: 'Hey, I can get an edge with this.'
That still continues today."

"There's always been people caught cheating," agreed
Bob Moore, a veteran motorsports journalist who began
covering stock-car racing for the *Charlotte Observer* in 1962.
"A lot of times, the punishment was just a slap on the wrist.
In some cases, like Dunnaway's, you get more than a slap on
the wrist."

And the man slapping the wrists would only reinforce his
authority in the 1950s, while those wanting to flout the law
were just starting to get warmed up. After just one season,
NASCAR founder Bill France changed the name of his
"Strictly Stock" series to Grand National, a name purportedly
lifted from an English horseracing event to make the series
seem a little classier. But whatever the name, stock-car racing was still a pretty crude sport to say the least, and its first

major stab at the big time proved as controversial as the first Strictly Stock race did.

When Darlington Raceway opened in 1950, it was billed as the sport's first superspeedway, an egg-shaped track 1.3 miles long and designed for high speeds, at least by the standards of the day. At a time when most races were run on small, grimy dirt tracks, Darlington was viewed as the first truly modern, purpose-built stock-car racing track.

Historians point to the track's Labor Day weekend opening for the very first Southern 500 as the birth of a new generation of tracks. But those who were there remember it as both rustic and a place where rules were liberally bent and sometimes broken.

Inspections were conducted before qualifying and away from the track, making it laughably easy to sidestep the rules.

"We hauled the car from Spartanburg [South Carolina], went to the racetrack first and signed in," recalled "Little" Bud Moore, a Congressional Medal of Honor winner who participated in the D-Day invasion in World War II and later won 63 races and three NASCAR championships as a car owner. "Then they took so many cars up there to inspection, then sent another bunch. Inspection was done before there was any practice. We were down there about a week going through inspection and getting all that stuff done before there was anything done at the track.

"They pulled the heads on the engine. Checked the compression. Checked the engine pretty thorough. Went through it pretty good. It had to be pretty stock. The only thing we were allowed to change on the chassis were the shock absorbers. We used heavy-duty shocks. Had heavy-duty hubs [on the axles]."

According to Bud Moore, it was a far cry from the high-tech scrutiny today's Winston Cup cars go through. "The inspection station was about two or three miles up the road, north from the racetrack. We drove the car up there. It went through inspection. And you drove it back to the racetrack," he said. "It was a concrete block building—a farm equipment building. They sold farm equipment. A pretty good-sized place. They moved all that out, and that's where they did the inspections. They didn't have any place in the infield of the track. No garage. No buildings. Didn't even have too good a rest room as far as that goes."

"They didn't have a man to follow you over there," remembered Jack Smith, who won 21 NASCAR races in a driving career that spanned the years from 1949 to 1964. "There were people that left that garage [after inspection] and drove the car on the highway and it didn't run good and they would stop and put another engine in it and go to the racetrack."

Although some racers took liberties with their engines, the winner figured out that the real secret to going fast was in the tires. "Johnny Mantz won the race in a Plymouth. We were in a Mercury," Bud Moore said. "Mantz won on Indy-type tires, Ward Riversides. Everybody else was running street-type tires. Sunday morning just before the race started they come out and put those tires on Mantz's car. He ran the whole race and never changed tires. I changed so many tires with a four-way lug wrench. Red Byron was driving a Cadillac for Red Vogt. They said they used 75 tires. We did go out in the infield and jack people's cars up and use their wheels and tires. Nobody realized [completing the distance] was going to take that many tires."

After the race, the second through fifth place finishers, Fireball Roberts, Red Byron, Bill Rexford and Chuck Mahoney, respectively, all protested the legality of Mantz's car, claiming it carried a bogus camshaft, shocks, and springs. But NASCAR President Bill France refused to have the car torn down after the race, because he was one of the four men who owned it. As if that wasn't bizarre enough, one of his co-owners was Hubert Westmoreland, the bootlegger and owner of Glenn Dunnaway's disqualified race-winning car from the first Strictly Stock race a year earlier.

NASCAR tech inspector Henry Underhill asked France to inspect Mantz's car after the race, but was told he could only look at it if he tore down the other 74 cars in the field first, which he obviously lacked the manpower and time to do. Underhill was so incensed he quit NASCAR shortly thereafter. It was neither the first nor last time that France was accused of manipulating the sport in his favor, and it's hard to claim that the events of the day were anywhere near fair. But France made the rules and again his will prevailed, no matter how much it angered and disgusted the other racers. France held all the power; the others could only hold their tongues.

Still, some on hand that day learned a thing or two, both about how France ran things and how to race. Mechanic and car owner Smokey Yunick was one of the quick studies.

"In 1955 Smokey went up to Firestone in Akron and wanted to go through the junk pile," remembered Lowe's Motor Speedway President Humpy Wheeler, who previously had been the tire company's racing representative in 1964. "Firestone always had a pile of tires that had been tried somewhere and didn't work. Smokey picked out four Indy-car tires that were harder compound, that were being discarded because they just were too hard. That's what he put on the '55 Chevrolet that Herb Thomas won the Southern 500 [at Darlington] in. Went 500 miles without a tire change. Was that cheating? No, it wasn't at the time, because the NASCAR tire rule was very loose."

Smith, meanwhile, had discovered some tire tricks of his own in the late 1940s and early 1950s. "People found out they could take tires, put them out in the sun, put them in an oven, soften the tires and put them on the left side or get a tire recapping company to do it," he said. "At the Peach Bowl Speedway in Atlanta, I found out that Jones Tire Company was a recapping company. I could get him to recap the tires for the left side and put [on] a certain compound and heat it to a certain temperature. It was just like day-and-night difference in how it handled. People always accused me of cheating on the motors. We didn't have to cheat on the motors. All we had to do was get the car to handling. Any way you could get tires heated to a certain temperature and then bring them out and cool them off, that made a difference. You could even use a kitchen-type oven."

Smith also saw firsthand how his competitors would try to get a good look at what he was doing. "Lee Petty. You could be sitting down beside your car. Here he'd come and lay down and start talking to you," Smith said. "And he'd be looking up under that car all the time he was talking to you. If you wrecked or something, he was going to come to see how bad it was. It wasn't that he was worried about you. He was looking for things on your car."

Others were trying similarly crude experiments in other areas of their cars, trying to make them go faster. Junior Johnson said he got his first taste of rudimentary aerodynamic engineering in the early 1950s with his whiskey haulers.

"I think it came from back when I was fooling with moonshine," he said of his eventual mastery of aerodynamics. "I messed around with cars, took the windshield wipers off. We used to bet money and see who had the fastest car on the highway. I could do a lot of stuff and pick up 15 to 20 miles per hour. You know a lot of cars had a big old hole where the headlights were? I'd flesh that out and stop it off. Just taking the wipers off would give you four or five miles per hour. Various things like that. Taking mirrors off. Once you pick up on that, you start seeing what makes a car not aerodynamic. Any time you help the aerodynamics of the car, you help the handling."

Humpy Wheeler, meanwhile, was looking for some help of his own in unlikely places, as he briefly and ultimately unsuccessfully pursued a driving career in the hardscrabble Southeast in the early 1950s. What he discovered was, to say the least, unorthodox.

"It seemed like the higher you got in racing the more sophisticated the cheating became. Years ago when I was trying to race—I was a teenager—I took this old Ford flathead down to Cowpens [South Carolina] Speedway, which on Friday night was hallowed ground in the Carolinas," Wheeler recalled. "It was what we called outlaw racing then. This was in the '50s. The best flathead racers in the South seemed like they would end up at Cowpens Speedway on Saturday night. The equipment was fairly simple. We all ran Mercury block engines. You were only allowed one Stromberg carburetor with one barrel. So everybody was always trying to monkey with that carburetor, but there wasn't much to it.

"There was one guy down there, though, his name was Black Cat, and he ran an appliance-white '34 Ford. He seemed to get more out of carburetors than anybody. So I wanted to buy a carburetor from this guy. He said, 'Let's go over to my house.' He didn't live far from the track. We went over to his house. It was a trailer. We went in there, and he went to the refrigerator and opened the door. It was full of Stromberg carburetors. They were cold. I paid the five extra dollars for one and put it on my car. And it ran better. What did he do to those carburetors? I don't know. He was very serious about the refrigerator, though."

Wheeler saw his share of fuel additives of questionable legality, potions designed to boost horsepower through more efficient combustion, a staple trick of cheaters throughout history. "There was a guy named Sweeney Prosser who sold something called 'Sweeney Prosser's Nitro X.' He sold it in five-gallon cans. It was a white can, but he had great graphics on the front. This was back in the '50s when graphics hadn't really come into racing big time," Wheeler said. "As soon as you saw that can, you had to buy it. It worked very well. Most people were running Amoco white gas then. What did he have in that fuel? Whatever he had, no one ever figured out. It did make the car run better. You could feel it in the car. When he died, so did the formula and the fuel. I never saw it again."

Even early in the sport's history, creativity mattered. And the further along the sport grew, the more creativity became a factor.

"If the other guy is doing well, competitors are always convinced that the guy is not better than they are, he's just a better cheater than they are." —Bob Moore

Chapter 2

Smokey was the worst or best,
I'm not sure what you'd call it.

—Ray Fox

The 1950s
Adolescent Rebellion

For the first half of the 1950s, the biggest story in NASCAR was Big Bill France himself. One by one, other rival sanctioning bodies fell by the wayside and France became the most important force in stock-car racing. Eventually, he'd become the most successful figure in American motorsports history.

In the early days, France's authority was consistently challenged, and just as consistently, those challenges failed. Big Bill decreed that racers who competed at races sanctioned by his competitors would be stripped of NASCAR points, which cost Lee Petty the Grand National championship in 1950. Several other top drivers of the day, most notably 1949 Strictly Stock champion Red Byron, Curtis Turner, and Bob Flock, would similarly run afoul of France and be stripped of points. Gradually, "Big Bill" consolidated control and power over the sport and all those who participated in it.

As the decade advanced, automobile factories quietly started to get involved in stock-car racing, often behind the scenes. In 1953, with France's blessing, they began supplying "severe usage kits," beefed-up suspension parts to better handle the rugged dirt tracks of the day. The change was made only after drivers and car owners complained bitterly about safety issues and the risk of death or serious injury due to mechanical failure.

These were stock cars after all, still driven to and from the races on public highways. The inspection process was still in its infancy and subject to change. A handful of inspectors looked over the cars to make sure they were stock. Engines were the only part of the car to receive any real scrutiny, unless a given team was winning too often or a particular driver or owner got on the wrong side of France. Then, anything could and frequently did happen.

France was free to either modify the rules or dispense his own particular brand of justice to benefit the sport. What most people didn't understand then (and still don't today) is that NASCAR's objective was to have close, competitive racing all the time. When that wasn't the case, France would change the rules or do anything else necessary to ensure the sport's survival. This was his business and his word was law, period.

"We went to a lot of races where they didn't have cars to fill the field," remembered Bud Moore, who like many of his contemporaries, figured out the score pretty quickly. "France would go down and get some rental cars and put numbers on them and tape up the headlights and put anybody in them to start the race. They did that many times. I don't think they were inspected at all. You could do a lot of fudging back then. But the thing was, if you ran in the top four or five they'd check you. You could run in the top 10 and not run in the top five and cheat like hell. NASCAR was just getting started. They were trying to put on a good show and draw spectators. They tried to do things right, to make things go as smooth as they could, yet they didn't want to really clamp on somebody really hard where they would lose him, because they needed every car and team they could get."

But like every rule about NASCAR, there were exceptions when France interceded and eventually drove people out of the sport. The first such episode began in 1955, with the unlikely arrival of an even more unlikely man to the world of racing.

Elmer Carl Kiekhaefer was born on June 4, 1906, in Cedarburg, Wisconsin. He was brilliant, detailed-oriented, paranoid, a visionary, an obsessive disciplinarian, and arguably the first truly professional racer, at least in the stock-car ranks.

Less than 10 years after the end of World War II, Kiekhaefer arrived at Daytona Beach and set the racing world on its collective ear. He was visibly out of place in the Deep South, a man who looked like a Hollywood caricature of a German Gestapo officer, with his crisp and spotless white uniform, rimless glasses, nearly bald head, puffy pink cheeks, and fat Cuban cigar.

Kiekhaefer had founded Mercury Outboards, a boat engine–manufacturing firm, in 1939, a business which would make him a multimillionaire. His sole motivation in entering NASCAR, or so he said, was to use the Grand National series to showcase his engineering brilliance in order to sell more boat engines.

Kiekhaefer arrived at Daytona with a fleet of Chryslers, all bearing the logos of his Mercury outboard engines on their quarter panels. He also used a car hauler, unheard of at the time, with the Mercury logo. At a time when racing crews truly looked like "grease monkeys," Kiekhaefer's team was clad in matching and immaculate white uniforms. He paid his drivers retainers of $1,500 per month and his crew members more than any other team.

And at Daytona, he managed to procure the services of free-spirited Tim Flock, the 1952 NASCAR Grand National champion. During the 1953 season, Flock carried a live rhesus monkey named "Jocko Flocko" as a passenger in his Hudson Hornet for 13 races, until the monkey got loose from his seat, costing him a victory at Raleigh, North Carolina, on May 30.

Flock had run afoul of France in 1954, when he was victorious in the Daytona Beach race, only to be disqualified for having an illegal carburetor. He also had been disqualified after winning the 1952 Daytona Modified race for using wooden roll bars, and vowed to quit racing after the 1954 fiasco. But one look at Kiekhaefer's gleaming, white 1955 Chrysler 300-C was all he needed to jump on board.

In those days, the Daytona superspeedway was still a gleam in Big Bill France's eyes. Instead, the competitors ran at the 4.1-mile Daytona Beach-and-Road Course, which as the name implied, covered both beach and road surfaces.

When Kiekhaefer and his band arrived in Daytona Beach, the competitors laughed at first, but not for long. Flock finished second to Fireball Roberts in the 1955 race. But Flock was given the victory after NASCAR Commissioner "Cannonball" Baker disqualified Roberts, saying the pushrods on his 1955 Buick had been illegally shortened .016-inch by mechanic Red Vogt.

But that was just the beginning. In 1955–56, the two seasons that Kiekhaefer's team would compete in racing, it won an astonishing 60 percent of the races it entered, 54 of 90, to be exact. By comparison, the second-winningest team in NASCAR history, Holman-Moody, won just 25.8 percent of the races it entered—and no other team, not Petty Enterprises or Junior Johnson or Hendrick Motorsports—has ever won more than 20 percent of its career races. Fans and rivals assumed Kiekhaefer was cheating, just as in later years, new generations would make the same unfounded claims about people like Richard Petty, Bill Elliott, and Jeff Gordon.

The truth behind Kiekhaefer's success was simple: He was better organized and better financed than any of his competitors. His outfit devoted far more men, more engineering expertise, more time, and more money to their operation than anyone else. Kiekhaefer spent more than $1 million on his race team, more than it cost to run a competitive Winston Cup team 30 years later.

"He was the first truly professional racing operation," said stock-car historian Bob Latford of Kiekhaefer. "Most of the tracks were still dirt then. He had a geologist who traveled with them to analyze the dirt surface of the track, what the composition was. He had meteorologists to study weather. He was one of the first to track air pressure, relative humidity, all of those kind of factors. He had uniforms for the crew. He transported the race cars by truck. He was just first-class. He out-factoried the factories."

In 1955, Flock won 18 Grand National races—including 11 wire-to-wire triumphs—and 18 pole positions, plus a record $37,779.60 in prize money. Kiekhaefer's cars won four other races that season, and finished one-two four times. Flock's single-season victory total would stand as a NASCAR record until Richard Petty broke it in 1967.

Flock's brother, Fonty, joined the Kiekhaefer fleet in 1955, as did archrival Buck Baker prior to the 1956 season. And Kiekhaefer often sponsored front-runners who drove for other teams. In the rival AAA circuit, Kiekhaefer's drivers won 10 of 13 races in 1955, with Frank Mundy scoring eight wins and Norm Nelson and Tony Bettenhausen one each.

Kiekhaefer's cars won an astonishing 16 races in a row in 1956—a record that surely will remain untouched forever—and 30 of 56 races during the year.

Still, the Kiekhaefer era would prove short, just two seasons. He vanished from racing never to return after the end of the 1956 season. His obsessive, militaristic ways drove team members and drivers crazy. Drivers were expected to observe bed checks and abstain from sex on the nights before races. Tim Flock, a fun-loving driver as most were back then, quit the team in early 1956, complaining of bleeding ulcers.

And fans bitterly resented the team's domination of the sport. In the mid-1950s, NASCAR was very much a regional, rural sport populated by hard-living and hard-racing characters. Kiekhaefer and his band of well-drilled crewmen in white jumpsuits simply didn't fit in. And fans weren't shy about letting him know it.

Kiekhaefer professed not to understand the animosity directed against him, such as the portrayal of him as a brutal, dictatorial caricature in both comic books of the day and the film *Thunder in Carolina*.

Even more troubling, perhaps, for Kiekhaefer were the internal NASCAR politics of the day. His success set a precedent that is still observed today in the Winston Cup garage: Win too much, and your cars will be virtually dismantled in post-race tech inspection. France even admitted as much. "Not once were we able to find any of Carl's cars illegal, and brother did we try!" he once said.

France's teardowns served three purposes: to satisfy race fans that Kiekhaefer wasn't cheating, to satisfy competitors that Kiekhaefer wasn't cheating, and intimidation. In spite of this, the racers of the day assumed that Kiekhaefer's success had to be because of cheating, not superior preparation or resources.

In many cases, those same people were cheating themselves, making their first crude attempts at manipulating engine size, playing with fuel additives, and beginning to tinker with aerodynamics.

"It got to where you couldn't believe what all happened," said racer Jack Smith. "You could have an engine that was too big. You could take a pint of whiskey and put it over there in his (the inspector's) toolbox and get by."

"All these things we got by with for a long time," said Bud Moore. "Everybody was doing it. You just did whatever you could get by with. NASCAR tried to do everything to keep it as honest as they could, but you weren't going to win if you were completely honest. You had to cheat. And the same thing is happening today. They've got a bunch of templates on the cars now, but they're still cheating. They're going to cheat somewhere, somehow. It's just harder to get by with stuff."

And not all the cheating was mechanical. Latford remembered one of his favorite episodes from the old Daytona beach-and-road course. "On the beach, I saw one of the great jobs of fudging," he said. "Back in the early days, the Modifieds used to line up five, six, seven across, and they'd send 'em off in waves in one-second intervals. Red Byron's car was starting in the very back of the field. Raymond Parks owned it. What they decided to do, Raymond always wore a nice brimmed hat. So he stood up on the sand dunes overlooking the pits, where they were taking off. And as soon as the first row of cars took off, Raymond took off his hat and waved it and that was the signal to the car all the way in the back. To the best of my recollection, there was 130-some cars that started that race and Byron led 'em all into the North turn. He got a running start."

Still, the man drawing the most attention was the one who either never cheated in the first place, or at least never got caught, despite NASCAR's best efforts.

"We'll go all the way back to the Kiekhaefer era," said journalist Bob Moore. "Kiekhaefer was the first real guy to come in as a car owner and dominate the sport. Everyone was convinced that his engines were illegal, his engines were bigger, his cars were lighter than everybody else's. Even though he had these huge Chrysler cars, everyone still thought he was lighter than everybody else. That's always the scenario: If the other guy is doing well, competitors are always convinced that the guy is not better than they are, he's just a better cheater than they are."

Even though the rule book hadn't evolved much at that point, NASCAR decided that Kiekhaefer's cars would undergo special scrutiny.

"A lot of races they would run one-two-three," Bob Moore said of Kiekhaefer's cars. "In those days, NASCAR would literally tear the car down. Not as scientific or detailed as it is today, but they did everything. They took the roll bars out and went through them and made sure they were legal. They went through them as detailed as they could be, trying to find out [if Kiekhaefer was cheating]. The same with the engines, they took 'em out, took 'em apart trying to find out if there were illegal camshafts, the carburetor was not what it was supposed to be. It's not like France allowed them to get away with it. If they were cheating, he couldn't find it."

"Kiekhaefer was torn down virtually every race, and they never could find a thing. He was such a perfectionist in his equipment," agreed Latford. "And everyone else accuses him of cheating, because they won't admit to themselves, they're just doing everything better than we are. They believe NASCAR's looking the other way—anything except, 'We're not working hard enough.'"

And the irony was, the guy who was straight had his cars ripped apart, while plenty of illegal ones sailed through with little or no attention. "They didn't have that many people inspecting back then," recalled former car owner and driver Cotton Owens. "One man was checking the engines and one or two checking the cars. By the time he checked 40 or 50 cars, you could do anything by the time they got back around."

If Kiekhaefer was an innocent wrongly villainized by the fans and even France in the mid-1950s, Smokey Yunick was just the opposite, a man who flouted every rule over a brilliant career and liked nothing better than to rub Big Bill's nose in it.

Like all truly great American heroes, Smokey Yunick was someone you couldn't invent, a man whose accomplishments dwarf even his formidable, larger-than-life mystique. In the annals of NASCAR history, he stands firmly where legend and fact collide, leaving onlookers to judge his impact for themselves.

A war hero who combined the brains of an engineer with a penchant for hard living and bacchanalian excess, Yunick was one of the most outspoken characters in NASCAR's history. He was by turns brilliant, profane, controversial, outrageous, and charming, a man who loved to stir things up and despised authority figures. He was one of the best and most honored mechanics in the history of stock-car racing and a pioneer in creative rules interpretation, a man who, along with Junior Johnson, reigned as an outlaw genius, rebel, and perpetual thorn in Bill France's side.

"Smokey was the worst or best, I'm not sure what you'd call it," said Ray Fox, who drove stock cars in the 1950s and was later a car owner and a NASCAR official. "He was always trying to get away with something. I think Smokey had the idea

[that] if you could have four things wrong and get one through, that was good."

In the half century of NASCAR's existence, Yunick stories have become the sanctioning body's equivalent of urban legends, wild tales some claim are gospel truth, while others dismiss them as apocryphal.

In short, he was an American original, someone the likes of whom we've not seen before nor will ever again. One hundred years from now, it's easy to imagine his ghost still walking through the Winston Cup garage, dressed in his trademark flattop Stetson and white overalls bearing a simple logo that reads "Best Damn Garage in Town."

• • •

Henry "Smokey" Yunick was born in Tennessee in 1923 and grew up in the outskirts of Philadelphia, where he dropped out of school in the 10th grade to support his mother and sister.

According to NASCAR historian Gene Granger, Yunick took up motorcycle racing in the late 1930s and got into aviation at about the same time. Both racing and flying would prove to be lifelong passions for Yunick. In fact, Yunick's nickname came from his early racing days, when his motorcycle began spewing smoke and the track announcer forgot his name and simply started calling him "Smokey."

When World War II broke out, Yunick became a B-17 pilot in the Army Air Corps, a stint that like many parts of his life would combine equal measures of achievement and controversy.

In a 1992 interview for *American Racing Classics*, Yunick recounted his first misadventure with the armed forces. "I went to the state fair in Memphis while I was stationed at Dyersburg [Tennessee]," he said. "I got drunk and came back for high-altitude formation. While I was up around 30,000 feet my appendix burst, but I didn't know what it was. I knew I needed to get on the ground in a hurry. After [the co-pilot] tried to land it two or three times and he couldn't, I came to long enough to get it on the ground. If I hadn't, we would all have been dead."

He recovered and became a highly decorated pilot, flying 52 bombing missions in Africa, Europe, Indochina, Burma, the Philippines, and Okinawa. He was wounded once and shot down over Poland on another occasion.

"I was in every World War II battle from Africa to Japan, every single one," Yunick said, though he conceded that maybe he wasn't quite suited to military life. "I was kind of a bad boy. I did about the same there as I did in NASCAR."

And a bad boy he was once he got back home from the war. Frustrated by the cold weather during a brief stint as a mechanic in southern New Jersey, Yunick hooked up his house trailer to his car and headed for warmer weather, following a remarkably similar path to NASCAR founder Bill France.

Yunick, like France, ended up in Daytona Beach, Florida, where each opened his own business: France a gas station and Yunick a repair shop known as the "Best Damn Garage in Town." Rivals in the auto-repair business, the men would soon butt heads in the racing world as well. It was a turbulent era and a time when Florida was known more as a rural frontier than a tourist mecca.

"If in 1947, I killed a guy in Daytona, unless he had five eye-witnesses, they wouldn't have bothered me," said Yunick, whose father-in-law was a district attorney in the area for a time. "I would have never even been arrested, 'cause I was wired in politically. They liked racers, and anything they could do for you they would.

"If a cop caught me in Georgia speeding and I could get away from him, I would never pay the damn speeding ticket and you could send all the telegrams and everything you want to Florida to get me extradited, and they'd just laugh about it, tear it up, and throw it away."

The heady days of the late 1940s and 1950s weren't quite as all-American as some historians would have you believe. According to Yunick, the racers raced hard and lived harder, partying with groupies he called "fence bunnies."

"As a rule, fence bunnies had a car, and they would circle our hotel like Indians circling a wagon train," Yunick said in an interview with reporter Juliet Macur of the *Orlando Sentinel*. "It wasn't uncommon for 10 or 15 couples to have sex in one room. If AIDS was around back then, we'd all be dead right now. . . . I'm not proud of what I did back then, but if a woman looked good, we didn't really abide by the Ten Commandments."

On the track, Yunick was as brilliant as he was wild off it. With Yunick preparing the cars, Herb Thomas won NASCAR Grand National (now Winston Cup) championships in 1951 and 1953, in addition to finishing runner-up twice. With Yunick as his mechanic and car builder, Thomas won 39 races over four years.

General Motors hired Yunick away in 1955 to help develop the legendary Chevrolet small-block V-8, an engine still in production today, albeit in a much modified form.

In the mid-1950s, Yunick began competing as an owner/crew chief in a limited schedule of NASCAR Grand National races. His most notable success came at Daytona, where he won four of the first eight major stock-car races at the famed speedway after it opened in February 1959. Fireball Roberts was the winning driver for three of those four races, including the 1962 Daytona 500. Yunick also dabbled successfully in open-wheel racing, winning the Indy 500 in 1960, when he served as Jim Rathmann's mechanic.

But Yunick's legend was built around his creative rules interpretation. He didn't just stretch the rule book, he bent it, broke it, and threw it out the window. And not only did he not like France, he had no use for NASCAR's chief technical inspectors, Norris Friel, Bill Gazaway, or Dick Beaty.

"Gazaway and his brother ran the inspections. The very best thing you could say for the both of them was they were first-class gas station attendants. I mean you're stretching it there," Yunick said. "Bill Gazaway was the chief inspector. If he had any claim to fame of any kind, it's that he was the finest reader of comic books there was in the United States. He had every issue of Superman and Spiderman and all that. To get in good with him, we used to go over there and get the latest comic books and throw them on his desk. He didn't know his ass from a hole in the ground.

"What was Friel's claim to fame? The best Model T mechanic in Washington, D.C. What was Dick Beaty's claim to fame? Dick Beaty was the best go-fer and odd-job guy that Eastern Airlines ever had in Charlotte. Not hardly a doctor in thermodynamics or anything, you know what I'm saying," said Yunick. "The people they chose to be inspectors were not qualified. And nobody who was qualified would have took the job because it didn't pay enough."

Yunick was equally blunt about how he stretched the rules. In fact, he claimed to have run an illegal supercharger for several years in the late 1950s, one of his most successful periods as a racer. "As far as cheating goes, they'll never stop it. There will always be some guy that'll think of something that's a little smarter than the average cat, but the reason there ain't any more of it on a big scale is that the only way it can be done successfully, only one person can know about it. And if there's only one person to know about it, like I was running supercharged Pontiacs and nobody knew about it. Nobody who worked for me knew it, had no idea that the engine was supercharged," Yunick said.

"And that's the only way you could get away with it. But what happened is it about goddamn killed me working day and night. I had to work on it when the other guys went home. Well, they didn't go home until one or two in the morning. Then I would start on building the stuff to supercharge the engines.

"The only reason the world never knew about it was I decided to stop doing it. I figured I'd used up all the good luck I had and got by with it for a couple of years, and figured, well, sooner or later somebody's going to figure out what happened.

So I abandoned it before I ever got caught," he said. "I made it to run off the flywheel and pressure plate. It's easy to make the pressure plate the compressor wheel, and it was inside a housing. It was easy to close it, and with urethane it was easy to get it down to a minimum size and so on. I'm not going to describe the whole thing to you, but it really was no big deal. It was something I thought about for years and years."

It's hard to imagine that Yunick actually ran this device without detection for a period of years. The purpose of a supercharger is to dramatically compress the flow of air through an engine, thereby sharply boosting horsepower. Even hidden in a bellhousing and run off a flywheel, the supercharger would have to have some way to direct air flow through the engine's intake system, something that surely should have been detectable to inspectors or, more likely, other competitors.

On the other hand, Yunick was so creative with other parts of the car that it's impossible to completely dismiss the story. His fellow competitors, for example, said Yunick was one of the first mechanics to really understand the relationship between the shape of a car's body and the effects of wind resistance at high speed.

Aerodynamics, in fact, was probably his true claim to fame on the scofflaw front. "Smokey was so far ahead of all of us in the aerodynamic downforce part of it. He could take a car and cut it all to pieces and work on it," said his contemporary Bud Moore. "There's no way we could have done some of the stuff he did."

"Smokey was real good. He did all kinds of stuff. He was smart," agreed David Pearson, the man who trails only

Richard Petty in career NASCAR victories. "He had a little spoiler put on top of it [his car] to keep air from getting down on it. You could see it, but you had to look at it close. It was back there at the rear window on the roof."

"You'd have to say Smokey Yunick was the best at the pre-1960 period. A lot of his was more innovation maybe than cheating. He knew where the gaps in the rules were, particularly as they related to engines," said Humpy Wheeler. "People used to say that Smokey couldn't make a car handle. Well, he could. The reason he got the handling rap was that his cars were going in the corners so much faster than everybody else. And it took a certain type of driver to drive for him because it was pretty intimidating. You couldn't come in and say, 'I don't have enough power.'"

"Some of the great [aerodynamic] innovations in those regards came from Smokey," said NASCAR historian Bob Latford. "Smokey was . . . running about a 15/16-scale car, just downsized so it made a smaller hole through the wind and therefore would be quicker. He used to take a half-inch out here and a quarter-inch out there and the car looks about the same until it's parked right next to another one that's actual [size]."

Like many of his peers, Yunick took umbrage at the term "cheating" even many years after his retirement.

"If you go back to 1950, you had the whole goddamn car to so-called be creative with. All right, now we've had 50 years of racing, 50 years of refining it, which are the collective efforts of all the smart people in the United States. And now the things that I would get disqualified for cheating before are absolutely legal today," said Yunick.

"The cheating thing is just like the law business. It depends on who's in power, the Democrats or the Republicans, and what part of the 19th or 20th or 21st century it is, because the laws are more and more abused the further we go. The lawyers are learning ways to circumvent the rules that we had yesterday. The same thing's happening in races.

"Ninety percent of the so-called cheating that was innovated, it wasn't cheating," Yunick said, citing as an example a Chevrolet he entered at the Daytona 500 in 1968. "There was no rule on how big the gas line could be. Everyone else ran a 5/8-inch gas line. That was adequate to supply the race engine with gas, no question about it. I chose to run a two-inch gas line, which was obviously much too big, but it was 11 feet long and it held five gallons of gas. Nobody ever [specified size]. A week after the race, the gas line couldn't be over a half-inch in diameter. The day that I did it, it was not illegal. That's how most all these innovations—so-called cheating—was not cheating the day it was done."

Still, he remained resolutely unconvinced that innovating can ever be effectively controlled by NASCAR. "They will find out there is no way to police creativity. No way in hell. There's always some guy who comes along like Ray Evernham that's smarter than the average cat, and he's going to figure out a way to get around it," said Yunick. "The difference between Gary Nelson's ability to think and Ray Evernham's—well, probably there's not a lot of difference in their IQs, but Evernham concentrates on engines and certain areas with a lot of expensive, very educated help. For 60 hours a week, he's studying new stuff to beat the rules. Gary Nelson is spending 50 hours a week trying to enforce the rules that were made yesterday. They're not even in the same game.

"The first inspector NASCAR ever had that even had a clue on what was going on is the guy they got now [Gary Nelson]. He's quite knowledgeable and should certainly be capable of doing a good job. But one of the problems is, and it's a very specific problem that will never go away, is that if he had, say four good assistants that are very knowledgeable and so forth, they're up against 100 mechanics factory-educated to like the third level, almost like doctors, you know what I mean?"

In their heydays, Yunick and Gazaway butted heads on many occasions, most notably at the 1968 Daytona 500, when Yunick was purported to have driven his race car away from inspection after NASCAR officials had removed the fuel tank.

The truth of what happened, to this day, remains somewhat shrouded in mystery, if only because Yunick has told and retold the story several different ways. But this much seems certain: Curtis Turner won the pole for the 1967 Daytona 500 in one of Yunick's Chevrolets, at a time when General Motors was not officially in racing, but rivals Ford and Chrysler were.

The pole victory for the unsponsored Chevrolet infuriated Ford and Chrysler, which at the time were pouring millions of dollars into racing, while GM's factory efforts had been curtailed.

"Smokey had been out of NASCAR for some period of time. He was primarily at Indianapolis, winning the race in 1960 with Jim Rathmann. He came back to Daytona in 1967," recalled Wheeler, who was there when it happened. "This was at the absolute height of the Ford-Chrysler factory wars, also between Firestone and Goodyear. In '65 and '66, Ford and Chrysler had boycotted, each one year. In '67 at Daytona they all were back. Chrysler had the mighty hemi, Ford had the 427 engine that was so good. Of course, there were no Chevrolets, hadn't been for some time, at least none of consequence on the big tracks. Smokey shows up with a '67 Chevrolet Chevelle with Curtis Turner driving. It was two renegades coming into Daytona, neither could care less about what anybody thought of them. All of a sudden, the first time I saw the car, I thought, the car is awful small. The Chevelle, an intermediate-sized production car, was smaller than the full-size Ford Galaxie and the Dodges and Plymouths that were running. But Smokey's car didn't look like it was as big as the Chevelles I'd seen.

"In practice it didn't really do much. Here comes pole day, and he wins the pole. This would be like a Peugeot coming in and winning the pole today in a stock-car race. It was such a shock. It was so embarrassing to the factory teams. I have never seen longer faces in my life at a racetrack, other than when somebody's killed, than at Daytona that day. NASCAR scrambled all around trying to find out who did what to whom, how did that damn thing get on the pole? It comes time for the qualifying races. Curtis on the pole and they drop the flag. He developed a mysterious smoke coming out of the car on the first lap. I guess Smokey said it was a blown engine or a leaky oil line. I suspect that he didn't want to show his hand. He knew that NASCAR was after him big time. The car didn't win the race, but probably in the history of stock-car racing there was never a bigger upset than what happened that day."

Ironically, because of rampant aerodynamic massaging by teams in 1965 and 1966, NASCAR brought templates to Daytona for the first time in 1967. These ran lengthwise from the car's hood to trunk and fit over the roof to make sure the trunk/roof/hood line was identical to production models. Yunick found an obvious loophole: NASCAR didn't measure how wide the car was, so he narrowed it. A narrower car pushes less air and, all other things being equal, it will be faster than a wider car.

"What did Smokey do with the car? He just made a small Chevelle out of it and took advantage of something nobody paid much attention to in those days, and that was aerodynamics,' said Wheeler. "It was less to move through the air. He had the fabulous ability to get more horsepower out of an engine than anybody else on Earth could. So the combination was earth shattering. As a matter of fact, that car was held in such high esteem as the ultimate cheater that it was sold for way up in the six figures at a collector car auction in Phoenix a couple of years ago. Somehow or other it miraculously showed up. Smokey verified to me that that was the Daytona car. It would be interesting to get that car and find out what size it really was."

Under pressure from France, Yunick agreed not to run the car for the pole in 1968, but would instead attempt to be the fastest second-round qualifier, which would still earn him prize money from a contingency sponsor. Yunick claims he cut the deal with France, which, in effect, would guarantee either Ford or Chrysler the pole for the season's most important race.

But the trouble started when Yunick showed up at tech inspection with his black-and-gold No. 13 Chevrolet Chevelle, which was now driven by Johnny Rutherford.

"That had a rubber fuel cell in it which was the legitimate size. They had it out about four times. It's a deal that had nothing to do with gas tanks. It had to do with Chrysler and Ford Motor Company telling France there wasn't going to be no unsponsored General Motors car sitting on the pole was what it was all about. So how do you want to approach that?" Yunick said at Charlotte in October 2000.

"The real story is a very complex story that had to do with politics and nothing to do with gas tanks. See, the year before that, I was an unsponsored car and it was a GM car. And it came out of nowhere and sat on the pole by about 4 miles per hour, OK? Which, apparently, they took as an embarrassment, Ford and Chrysler. General Motors still hadn't come back in the thing in '68. And so the deal still went: There won't be a GM car on the pole. That's what happened. There's a lot more to the story. The car never ran. Nobody knows whether it would have sat on the pole or not. And in June, Firestone wanted to do a tire test at Daytona and they hired me to do it. Five days before the tire test, when NASCAR discovered that Firestone was going to use my car for the tire test, they banned it. They said, 'You can't do no tire test here, either.' That was it."

Well, most of it anyway. There was an angry confrontation in tech inspection. "We had the gas tank checked, and we were in inspection. They checked me and thought I had a secret gas tank someplace. Then they said, 'You gotta go back to the chief inspector.' He had a list of 11 things that had to be fixed before the car could run. Item number one was replace homemade frame with stock frame. Now, you've got an hour and a half left, then you've got 10 more things.

"So, I said, 'Well, you've got about 10 minutes to decide if you're really serious about this thing, because 10 minutes from now, if you don't come over and tell me the car was passed in inspection, I'm leaving.' They never came over.

"And then when I went to leave, I wanted to drive the car out and I wanted to put gas in it. And the inspector said, 'You can't move this car, 'cause we're not done inspecting it.'

"I said, 'Don't make any difference, I'm leaving.' Well, I wasn't having any luck with him, so I knocked him on his ass, went and got in the car, and let my boys tow me back, and then I decided to go round the track one time with the car. Then I had that big rope on it and I thought, no that won't work, I'm liable to run over that damn thing. So we just took it home. That's all there was to it."

Except, of course, for the fact that the black-and-gold Chevrolet had a two-inch, 11-foot-long fuel line that held five gallons of gas, a feature that would be outlawed a week later.

"Smokey was a genius in his time. He was as good as anybody was during his time," said Charlie Gray, a retired engineer who was Ford Motor Company's program coordinator for stock-car racing from the early 1960s through 1970. "He was a great power in his day. He certainly made his mark, and he deserved every bit of the recognition he got."

"Smokey was an extremely talented, highly educated mechanic," agreed car owner Leonard Wood, co-owner of the legendary Wood Brothers racing team. "He used a lot of common sense and was innovative."

•　　•　　•

But for all his technical brilliance, the fiery Yunick had a hard time coping with the politics of automobile racing and the politics of the automobile manufacturers. And that led to his retirement from NASCAR in 1971.

"The politics were a big part of it. When we got going in the 1950s, [France] in his head wanted to keep the cars absolutely stock, which was totally impossible for safety reasons, not speed reasons. That's how the cheating got started, to keep from getting killed."

The weakest link in the 1950s stock car was the front-end spindle, which held on the wheel assembly and connected it to the steering and suspension. As speeds began to increase, the g-forces and loads on the spindles increased, too. Eventually the spindles would fail, and the result would be wrecks, sometimes with catastrophic results. "He forced us to cheat in the beginning to make heavier spindles," Yunick said of France's attempt to keep the cars strictly stock. "The factories at that time, they would make a bigger [spindle] for you."

Yunick knew that France held all the cards and there was little anyone could do, least of all a renegade car owner who openly voiced his displeasure with NASCAR's boss.

"If he wanted to disqualify the car, he could. It was his out-fit, and nobody made me run in the thing, so if he abused what I thought was his power, I figured, well, it's his outfit, and if I can't handle the heat, I need to go somewhere else," Yunick explained.

"I ran the Ford Torino Talladega [a limited production model] in 1970 at Daytona, and they forced me to run a Ford that was four inches higher than the other ones. They knew where the cheating was going on and they watched everybody else and they caught everything on mine, and you could see my car was sitting that much higher up in the air.

"I said, 'Well, you only get to do that one time.' And I told them before the race I said, 'You make me race this way, this'll be the last time I ever race in the South.'

"He [France] said, 'Ah, you'll be back.'

"I said, 'If you don't think I'm gone, you count the days till I get back.' And I said, 'If I see you first, I'll get on the other side of the street, and if you see me, you get the fuck on the other side of the street. You want to know what time of day it is, it'll cost you 100 bucks'. That's the way he left it. When I left, Junior Johnson was the next one that got my place, and they worked his ass off till they run him off. You can only take that so long."

Yunick never again would compete as a car owner or mechanic at a NASCAR race. Although he frequently showed up at races in the years ahead, he battled bone cancer and a host of other ailments and was absent from the scene for most of the 2000 season, until showing up at Charlotte in October for the UAW-GM Quality 500.

"I was diagnosed with everything but pregnancy," Yunick said with a raspy laugh as he sat in the infield media center at Charlotte in October 2000. "Finally, about a month ago, I took all the medicine there was and threw it in the trash can, told the doctor, 'I'm done with this shit. If I'm going to die, I'm going to die. Don't even talk to me about it anymore.' I picked up horsepower, about 70 percent. I feel 100 percent better. I came away from wheelchairs, those things you push, canes. Now I'm walking by myself—all that in 20 days.

"I just went up and down. I didn't know what was happening. I was so weak I couldn't do nothing. I really didn't want to live because I couldn't do nothing. I'm starting to get back in the ball game. I may be going to drop dead because I won't take the medicine, but I ain't taking no more. If I'm going to die, let's get it over with. I'm headed for 78 now, and I've had enough of everything, with no regrets. I had a good life."

And just as he refused to obey authority in the military or NASCAR, Yunick wasn't about to take a doctor's word on how to live. He lived his entire life on his own terms and vowed to finish it the same way. He died May 9, 2001.

"I think he was years ahead of his time in some of the aerodynamic things," said Barry Dodson. "One of the Chevelles he had is up in Richard Childress's museum now, and every time I go over there I take time to look at that car. I think how could anybody have that mind and that ingenuity 20 years before anybody else, before we had the use of the wind tunnels and all the data that we have from the manufacturers? He was way, way ahead of his time."

The lowered nose on the "Yellow Banana" Ford Galaxie built by Junior Johnson (at middle right) was obvious, as were the chopped roof and raised tail. Yet NASCAR inexplicably let the car compete in Atlanta in 1966 in a controversy-filled race. (Don Hunter)

Chapter 3

The cheating as we used to call it was fun. It was a little bit like outrunning the police with a V-8. It was fun. It didn't hurt anybody.

—Robert Yates

The 1960s
Age of Experimentation

To hear veteran racers tell it, clichéd as it sounds, the 1960s really were a simpler time for NASCAR mechanics and crew chiefs. With only a skeletal rule book and inspection process to deal with, car builders were given wide latitude in how they prepared their race cars. And they used it.

France had gradually conceded that his notion of running strictly stock cars was impossible. As NASCAR slowly evolved from half-mile dirt tracks to ever-larger paved tracks and the Big Three automakers engaged in a horsepower war to build faster cars, race speeds increased tremendously, which forced teams to structurally reinforce their cars for safety's sake.

Race teams discovered quite by accident that if they beefed up suspensions and chassis for safety, the cars had less chassis flex and deformation at speed, which meant they handled better. And if they tinkered with the dimensions of the chassis and body, there were additional incremental performance benefits to be gained.

"It was a lot more of an individual sport a long time ago when it first started," remembered seven-time Winston Cup champion Richard Petty. "When it first started it was strictly stock cars, then somebody said, 'Why don't we put bigger springs in it?' or bigger shocks or bigger tires, whatever it was. Then somebody said, 'You know, if we cut this window here, cut this fender.' There were no templates, so we'd just do it. Make the cars longer, shorter, narrower, higher, sideways, whatever it was. We used to run with no spoilers, so that was something that they [NASCAR] didn't have to check. They didn't have any templates. They checked the weight of the car and the height of the car and that was about it. Used to be we come down here, in an hour you used to do inspections. If you wasn't just really, really cheating bad you were OK."

"Inspections were very simple," added reporter Bob Moore of the *Charlotte Observer*. "They would look at the body. There was no such thing as a template. The engine size was checked for cubic inches. The body was looked at, so your fenders weren't too low in this part or that part. But again it was all visual, eyeballing it. There was a stick that was run under the car to make sure you weren't too low. There was a certain height you had to be, and there was a measurement for that. It was pretty basic. There was no science to it, but most of the inspectors had a fair amount of mechanical knowledge, so if a spring was wrong or a carburetor was offset or whatever, you'd have to fix it.

"In the '50s and early '60s, the whole idea was there was a lot less written down. There was a lot more gray area then than there is now. And the whole ability of a crew chief, or a mechanic—because in the '50s and early '60s, there was no such thing as a crew chief—was, how far in the gray area can you go to outrun your opponent?" Moore said. "Even in the early '60s, when Norris Friel was NASCAR's technical director, he'd say, 'OK these are the things that you have to do, these are the things we're going to check. Now we know you may go beyond this area, so watch it. We may even let you go beyond the area, but if you get too far or too big an advantage, we're going to take it away.'"

The atmosphere, while competitive certainly, was far more collegial and less cutthroat. Creativity was a staple of the stock-car racing experience.

"Part of the enjoyment was, how far can people go? How innovative can you get? There's always been people caught cheating. In some cases you get more than a slap on the wrist. But a lot of times, it's just a slap on the wrist," said Moore. "As long as you didn't go too far, you got away with it. You just kind of turned your backs. But if the guy you're competing against thinks you're getting away with too much, he'll go to the officials and say, 'This guy is half a second faster than everybody. There's got to be a reason why.'"

Petty advocated a philosophy he called "cheat neat," which meant trick up your car, but not so blatantly as to draw the ire of NASCAR officials. "The big deal was cheat neat, you know what I mean?" Petty said. "Or cheat on 15 things and do two or three things that's very obvious. NASCAR'd catch them, and they was happy as June bugs. You got through with what you wanted to get through with."

Petty was one of several masters of experimentation in the 1960s, along with fellow NASCAR legends like Leonard Wood, Smokey Yunick, and Junior Johnson. And experimentation was the keyword of the day. Making stock cars go fast in those days was much more of a hit-or-miss process and much less scientific than it is today.

There were no computers or digital equipment to test with. When drivers arrived at Daytona for the first time in February 1959, for example, they were shocked to learn that cars ran around the mammoth 2.5-mile track faster together than they did alone. And no wonder the racers were surprised: They were used to banging fenders on half-mile dirt tracks at 60 mph, not running 140 mph around a superspeedway. They'd never been exposed to drafting or how to use it to their advantage.

But they figured it out quickly. "When we started running Daytona, that was the beginning of really trying to streamline for wind resistance," said former owner/driver Cotton Owens. "We didn't know anything when we went to Daytona in 1959. No one knew you could go out there and draft faster with two cars than with one until we actually did it in the race. I set fast qualifying time at 143 miles an hour, but that was absolutely a stock automobile, with a stock engine. Even at that speed, my car would actually raise the front wheels off the ground going in the corners. We didn't know how to keep it down. Of course, we learned. Dropping the front end down, raising the rear end. Went back in 1960, we were already dropping the front ends on them. Just learned from trying it. Somebody showed up with a car all propped up in the rear and ran fast, and it was on then. Everybody copied it."

And they tried other tricks as well. "Everybody was doing different things," recalled driver David Pearson, Richard Petty's main rival. "I remember the Pettys came to Daytona in 1960 or '61 and Lee had a car with a vinyl top on it. Looked like a golf ball. They said a golf ball will go through the air good, so that should. Even back then people were trying different things with aerodynamics. You didn't know as much then because they were just starting superspeedways. I heard all my life that the lighter a car is the better it is, and naturally the lower it is the better the air will go over it. If air went under the car, it would pick it up. At places like Daytona when we first started there, we'd find out that the car would be tight coming off the corner. What it was doing was picking the front end up with air getting under it. So they started lowering the front end. It was a lot of experimenting, seeing what would work, learning about it."

"In February 1960, I went to Daytona. I'd go down the back-stretch in my '60 Pontiac and spin the wheels," said Jack Smith. "I told the mechanics, and they said the car wasn't streamlined enough, that all I was doing was running up against a wall and pushing the wall. Then two years later Ford Motor Company realized they could not run their cars through the air. Ford hired [chassis builder] Banjo Matthews. Banjo took the car and cut the floor pan out of it, lowered the car about four inches, changed the contour of the windshield. Then they found out that Ford would run. The word got out quick, and pretty soon Banjo had orders to build more race cars than he could do. He was the first one I ever knew that cut down or streamlined the cars. This was '62 or '63 at Daytona."

Some of the teams had particularly inspired ways to get the noses of the cars down, which was vital for success at Daytona, as well as other new tracks that were built in the 1960s at

Charlotte, Atlanta, Michigan, and Rockingham, high-speed facilities that were inexorably replacing the old, slow dirt tracks.

"Joe Gazaway, [a NASCAR inspector and brother of chief inspector Bill Gazaway] came over once when we were down at Daytona in the mid-'60s. I think we were getting ready to qualify," said Bud Moore. "The Wood brothers had their car there. They had put the tarp over it. Leonard had some turnbuckles under the hood. He'd get under there and pull those turnbuckles and pull the front end closer to the ground and make it run faster. Joe happened to see his feet sticking out from under there. He picked the tarp up and smiled. He said, 'Lenny, what do you think you're doing?' That was the biggest laugh."

"In 1962 or '63 you began realizing that dropping the top of the grille a little bit lowered everything on the front end," recalled Wood. "All that stuff was figured out pretty early. Ford used to have a stack of shims under the radiator cradle, about an inch or so. It was really easy to take that stack of shims out and drop the nose an inch. It didn't change much. There wasn't a whole lot of that drooping the nose anyway. If you drooped it too much, you could visually tell it."

"Leonard made a lot of stuff with his hands," said Pearson. "He'd take the parking light areas and bend them in a little, just for aerodynamics. I got on to him one time when I was driving for Holman-Moody. His car was behind me, and I told him the front bumper looked like a nail coming at me the way he had it pointed right in the center. They would do things like that. Anything to get the air to flow a little better."

The Chrysler contingent, led by the Pettys and Owens, had their own tricks, unique to the torsion-bar front suspension that Dodges and Plymouths used. "Once it became obvious that getting the car low was a good thing at Daytona, people started working on it. They dropped the sheet metal down on the nose, lowering it any way they could and still get by," said Owens. "On the Chryslers, on the lower control arm, you had an adjusting screw. It went up into another arm that held the car up through the torsion bar. We had some [wooden spacers] that would bust when you went in the corner and would automatically drop the front end a full inch. Then when we couldn't get away with that we started machining the bolts and putting little Allen screws in them to let them fall down so far. On the rear they had an anchor back there. We'd slot those bolts to where it could come down so far just from the pressure of the car being on the track. It would automatically lower. It would hold them up long enough to get through inspection. You could just about jump up and down on the front end yourself, and it would automatically come down. The first little bump it got on the track would lower it. It would mean the difference of an inch or an inch and a half, and at Daytona that was a second or a second and a half on the track."

Owens also borrowed a popular trick from drag racers of the day, swapping the heavy sheet-metal fenders and hoods for lightweight aluminum, which also helped handling. "We got away with that for a little bit," he admitted. "Then the first wreck where it was actually seen that it was used, they [NASCAR] outlawed it. It was better because it was lighter. You could take all the sheet metal off the front end and put aluminum up there. You couldn't tell the difference in it, from aluminum to sheet metal. You painted it just like it was sheet metal. Front fenders, hood, bumpers. We were always busting the right front tire. So we got a lot of weight off it. That's where it really helped. It put more weight to the rear of the car."

"Everybody was going wide open trying to change aerodynamics," agreed Junior Johnson. "That simply came about because they had found about all the horsepower they could find. They had to go somewhere else. The easiest horsepower you ever found in your life is in the body."

On the smaller tracks, fertile minds were also at work in the early 1960s. "Rex White ran short tracks with his car all lowered to where it was only about two inches off the ground on the left side and about six or seven inches on the right side," said Owens. "Everybody saw him get around those tracks real good, so they started copying it. That brought on what we called the idiot stick. NASCAR used that to measure ground clearance under the car and wouldn't let you get any lower than that stick. They slid it underneath the car. That's how they measured them for height until, I guess, the '70s, when they started measuring it from the roof."

"Anybody could fudge the rules, but what you wanted to do was come up with something that was in the limits but was very beneficial to you," said car owner Leonard Wood of how the teams worked in the 1960s. "Come up with something that nobody else has even though it's legal. Then it depends on how big a secret you wanted to keep. You didn't tell anybody anything. If somebody let you know something, you might help them. You'd tell him enough to pacify him but not everything that made it go fast. And that's what he'd do to you. If you were running a Ford and so did Bud [Moore] and Junior [Johnson], each one wants to look good. You weren't out there to make Bud or Junior look good. They were your competitors, too. You wanted to beat them as bad as anybody. You could share a little of this or that, but you never told him how to really make it go."

The bigger, faster tracks and the aerodynamic innovations of the early 1960s had some chilling, unintended consequences. For one thing, longer tracks and more aerodynamic cars meant speeds rose sharply, and with those speeds danger increased exponentially. In 1964, three of the sport's most popular drivers, Joe Weatherly, Fireball Roberts, and Jimmy Pardue lost their lives in separate crashes. When races were 100 miles on dirt tracks, gas mileage and fuel capacities weren't an issue. But when the races became 500 miles long, suddenly teams began illegally hiding fuel wherever they could find a place in the car, at grave danger to the drivers.

This led directly to the development first of the rubberized fuel cell in 1964 and then the purpose-built stock-car frame and roll cage, which was developed by Holman-Moody in 1966, approved by NASCAR, and is in fact similar to the chassis still used today. The Holman-Moody chassis/roll cage unquestionably was a huge improvement from a safety standpoint, but it was, for all intents and purposes, the end of true stock cars and the beginning of stock-appearing cars that can only be driven on a racetrack. And the less cars were stock, the more people were tempted to cheat them up, especially when it came to weight, fuel, and aerodynamics.

Journalist Bob Moore recalled one such example from the early 1960s. "One of the teams basically had extra gas stored in the car for every race. They went the whole season putting in extra gasoline at every race. It'd be different places, different times, because the competitor might find out where you had it hidden, they'd go and tell NASCAR, they'd check and it wouldn't be there," he said. "This particular race team was extremely smart, extremely innovative, and they'd use every single way to hide gasoline you could possibly think of. Frame rails, roll bars, in the fuel cell, in the dashboard, wherever they could get it so that it would flow into the carburetor or the gas tank and give them an extra one to three gallons of gas."

Racer Jack Smith said he saw rivals hollow out front cross-members, the center support that runs under the engine joining the left and right sides of the frame together, to hold extra gasoline. "They'd weld that up and take and run the fuel line like it was going through the side of the cross-member, but they'd hook it up to the cross-member, which had gas in it. And there were some that tried to put it in the roll bars."

"They checked the fuel cells pretty closely. Couldn't hold but 22 gallons," added Bud Moore. "We all had a little gimmick going. Some of them had gas in the roll bars.

"Some had it here, some had it there. I did mine a little different. When we went through inspection, they checked the fuel cell and sealed it all up. I waited until a certain time and stuck an air hose in it and blew that jewel up and made it bigger. They never took the fuel cell back out of it after they checked it. I just put the air hose to it. Blow the cell container, stretch it. I'd get a gallon, gallon and a half, sometimes two more gallons in it."

Crewman Barry Dodson would later use a similar trick when he worked for Petty Enterprises in the early 1970s. "We'd come here to Daytona. We always had the end garage stall. I'd hide in the trunk and open up the fuel cell to where it held two more gallons than it was supposed to. I'd tap on the quarter panel, and they'd open up the trunk and get me out," he said.

Still, some car owners drew the line at what they would do with fuel. "Putting fuel in roll bars, I never did it because it was bad enough to have fuel in the rear of the car, much less having it up there around you," said Cotton Owens. "But some people made special bars for the left door and put it in there. To me that was crazy, because the driver was sitting right there with it. You could hide three or four gallons like that, and that could make the difference between winning and losing. They had it rigged so it would free-flow from there into the tank. After they ran so long they had a valve they'd trip and let it run in the tank."

Historian Bob Latford recalled one fuel-related incident that involved one of NASCAR's most time-tested tricks: replacing an illegal part with one even more flagrantly illegal. "One time at Martinsville, Holman-Moody's car that Fred Lorenzen drove got caught. It was supposed to be a 22-gallon gas tank, and there was 22.9 gallons or something like that, and they made him take it out and take it away. And the team fussed and fumed and did the work, and they put a 28-gallon tank back in. They never checked the one they replaced it with."

Arguably the funniest stories of all came from David Pearson, not in a NASCAR race but when he was driving for Bud Moore in the Trans-Am road racing series in the late 1960s. "When I drove Bud's car one time I had some tires with water or lead in them. I go through inspection with those tires and then turn around and switch them [with lighter tires] or punch a hole in and let the water out," said Pearson. "And he had a gas tank at Riverside [California] that all the fuel wouldn't come out of when they drained it. They had a thing up in it that would just let so much of it drain out. So the inspectors told Bud that he had to get all the fuel out of the tank before they came back. So he got a bunch of the guys on the team to stand around the car and pee on the ground so it looked like they had drained all the fuel out."

The Trans-Am series was also where one of Smokey Yunick's most infamous cars surfaced, this one a 1968 Chevrolet Camaro. "While Number 13 may look like a '68 Camaro, it has most certainly been 'massaged,'" noted *Hot Rod* magazine in a 1996 retrospective. "Acid-dipped body parts abound, the front sheet metal drooped, all four fenders were widened, the front subframe was Z'd to lower the car, the floor pan was moved up, the windshield was laid back and thinner safety glass was used throughout the car. The list of tweaks is endless. Smokey even pulled the drip rails in closer to the body! ... The engine was fitted with a pressurized, quick connection that allowed the driver to quickly add oil to the engine from the interior during pit stops. Because the driver was an active participant during pit stops in the cockpit, a cable-ratchet mechanism from a military helicopter was used to release the shoulder harness so the driver could perform his necessary tasks."

Another popular "innovation" of the day—although admitted hardly as exotic as some of Yunick's tweaks—was lead, or more specifically how the heavy metal was used. In an effort to make cars lighter in race trim, crew chiefs over the years would make replica car products out of lead and replace them with the real articles after the car went through inspection.

"I've seen everything from lead radios to lead watercoolers. Everybody's tried to cheat on weight. Weight used to be a big thing," said Richard Childress, who began racing in the 1960s as one of the so-called "independents," small-budget, small-resource teams who had little chance of beating the well-funded teams like Petty's. "There's so many different stories you could tell. There was a team one time that was running lead inside the wheels on the right side. This was when we had the weight situation. Those tires and wheels would each weigh about 50 pounds extra. And to watch those guys pick those things up and come back around the car with 'em on the first pit stop was pretty amazing. That was the slowest pit stop of the day for those guys."

Latford said he saw teams make race weight by filling their tires with water and then changing them during early pit stops. Like Childress, he also saw plenty of lead parts, too. "A lot of guys used to put water in their tires before they rolled across the scales to give 'em weight. Then after they went over 'em, they'd change tires," Latford said. "A team was caught with a radio in their car that looked like a regular radio, but it was made of solid lead. They used to put Thermos bottles in the cars and fill 'em with mercury, before they figured out how dangerous it could be."

In fact, the lead trick was one that stayed in fashion for several decades. In a 1988 interview with *NASCAR Winston Cup Scene's* Deb Williams, NASCAR Competition Director Dick Beaty showed off a virtual gallery of confiscated lead parts, including a replica of a fuel filter that weighed 60 to 70 pounds. Another was an oil tank full of lead.

"That thing must weigh 200 pounds," Beaty told the racing publication. "When the cars were weighed only once, that was placed where the oil tank would be located, complete with lines running to it. As soon as the car was weighed, the lead-filled oil tank would be removed and the true oil tank placed in the car." Beaty said he had also caught teams using lead goggle holders and, in one instance, a lead helmet, which sat in the car while it was weighed and was exchanged after the inspection.

"I had a helmet one time that had lead in it. I've still got it," Pearson admitted. "You'd just switch helmets. That thing must have weighed 50 pounds. You just left your helmet in the car when they weighed it, then wore another one in the race."

Then there was the ever-popular buckshot method of lightening one's car, a method that saw occasional use from the late 1950s until the early 1990s. "I remember people coming in a shop near mine in Spartanburg [South Carolina] and buying a thousand pounds of gunshot," said Jack Smith. "They'd take them and put them in bags and put them in the car right inside the quarter panel or in the doors. They'd have a lever up under the dash or on the side looking like a door handle, connected to a knife that would get the bags open. Underneath the bags would be holes, and the gunshot would roll out on the track. First thing you know, other cars would hit the fence because the lead shots were going out and getting in the racing groove."

Smith professed admiration for the creativity of Junior Johnson. "Junior had one of the best things I ever seen. Somebody on his team brought a two-gallon water jug. Somebody in Tennessee had shown him something, a liquid metal of some sort. It wasn't mercury; it was something heavier than mercury. They filled that jug up and put it in the car. They'd weigh the car. Right before the race this old boy would put that one up and put a real water jug in there. It'd lighten the thing 200 pounds. Everybody had a water jug in their car. Man, you take that much weight off, it's a lot."

As flagrant as this all seems today, at the time nobody made too much of a deal about other guys cheating, as long as it didn't get too far out of hand. "This has always gone on," said Bob Moore. "The whole thinking to the deal was, even at the beginning when they came up with the first set of rules, these are the rules, but we understand you may go beyond these rules. We'll let you go beyond them to a certain point, then we're going to cut your hand off. The driver's ability could make up a lot of difference. And that was part of what made the beginning more creative, rambunctious, interesting. You never knew from week to week who was playing a game, who was cheating here, who was cheating there. You'd learn what this guy was doing and then you did it. The idea was, you try to be the first and let them catch you."

"The cheating, as we used to call it, was fun. It was a little bit like outrunning the police with a V-8. It was fun. It didn't hurt anybody," said Robert Yates. The son of a Baptist minister in North Carolina, Yates worked his way up from a gofer at Holman-Moody in the early 1960s to the owner of a two-car Winston Cup team led by 1999 Champion Dale Jarrett. "We used to have a deal where you couldn't close off your grille. Banjo Matthews was great at getting a grille small. We finally learned that the more you tape them off the faster they would go. So we put this plastic door screen back in behind there. Joe Gazaway, he would start looking in the grille. It was his job to inspect the grille and make sure you didn't have any kind of blockage in it. One time we put a water bottle with a pump on it and a nozzle so when he stuck his head down in there we shot him right between the eyes. It was that kind of a fun deal."

"I think the reason for the creativity was what you'd call shade-tree engineering, where people actually worked on their own cars pretty much," said Martinsville Speedway's Dick Thompson. "I know the Wood Brothers used to do a lot of experimentation themselves and were way ahead of a lot of people. Sometimes you'd see another mechanic walk over to the car and start to get down on his hands and knees and start to look under the car, and they would just say in a very quiet voice but very menacing, 'Don't look under there.'

"In those days, when a team brought cars to the racetrack, each car was pretty much individual," Thompson continued. "They're kind of cookie cutters today. Everybody's using the same roll cage, the same this and that.

"Basically, everybody doing their own engineering was saying, 'Let's see what I can get away with,'" said Thompson. "They were pushing the limit. NASCAR really had to watch things. Even after you went through inspection, they had some tricks up their sleeve. There were times when the so-called independents bought a factory car and they would sit down and [review the hidden features of the cars] with the previous owners. There would be switches on that car they had no idea what they went to."

Many times, those switches would be used to operate hydraulic pumps that would lower the car on the track and raise it before inspection. "Jim Hurtubise, at Riverside one time, they were using lowering devices on the car, little microcranks," said Latford. "He got in the car at the start-finish line and was getting ready to start the car. You used to have starter buttons. He put his hand up. The switch was down here, and the car started to fall."

Latford saw plenty of other tricks, too. "There was the old thing of putting wood or charcoal in the springs before they'd go out to qualify. And of course, the first bump you hit, the charcoal or wood would fragment, and there'd be splinters down on the apron of the first turn, but you couldn't prove where it came from, so there was nothing you could do," he said. "The other trick was freezing the shocks at the desired height. And after it pushed out in line and sat there, it would thaw, the car would settle and away they go."

Bud Moore used a similar trick. "We had pieces of plastic that we'd stick underneath the springs to hold the car up," he said. "We'd take stones and stick them underneath the springs in the front and let them down real easy. The rocks would hold the springs up through inspection. Then when you had the first bump the springs would crush the rocks and let the car drop."

According to Martinsville's Thompson, the acknowledged master of chicanery in those days was Junior Johnson, a man who grew up in the hardscrabble country of Wilkes County, North Carolina, and had served time in a federal prison for running moonshine. Johnson, whose rugged persona and hard-ass driving style would later earn him icon status as the subject of Tom Wolfe's magazine profile, "The Last American Hero," knew every trick in the book. And he had a very fundamental attitude about breaking the rules, one he explained in an interview with the *Orlando Sentinel*'s Juliet Macur in 1998. "With the rules in those days, it was easy to cheat," said Johnson. "You just worked on what NASCAR didn't check. If they didn't check your gas tank, you had a bigger gas tank. If they didn't check your engine, you had a bigger engine."

Of course, Johnson would bend the rules even on the parts that NASCAR did check. "I think the funniest thing I ever saw, I was watching a race at Bristol one time in the late 1960s, watching Junior Johnson drive, and I had my binoculars on Junior," remembered Thompson. "It seemed like when he'd come out of the pits, going down the backstretch, the car would drop down. But every time he'd come in to make a pit stop, NASCAR would run out, stick that measuring stick under his car, and it was totally legal. As he went out, then, the car would start lowering. It turned out later on that he had hydraulics in there, and he could lower the front end."

"The cheating, being innovative, Junior was noted for it," Latford added. "He didn't break the rules; he just found things that were not covered by the rules. He'd find a space between the lines, so to speak, and do things that weren't covered. Then they'd come up with another rule to cover it, and he'd have to go do something else."

Well, maybe that isn't exactly accurate, because Johnson might be best known for building a car that was blatantly illegal, so completely beyond the spirit of the rules, let alone the letter of the law, that he earned himself a permanent spot alongside Smokey Yunick in the NASCAR scofflaws' hall of fame.

The year was 1966, the place the old Atlanta Raceway. NASCAR was in the midst of one of its darkest eras, thanks to a battle of wills between Big Bill France and the Big Three automakers in Detroit, who were locked in a rapidly escalating horsepower war and were trying to bring ever-more-radical power plants to stock-car racing.

A year earlier, Chrysler had launched a NASCAR boycott that lasted about half a season, after France banned the automaker's omnipotent 426 hemi engine because it was far more powerful than any rival production engine from Ford or General Motors. Without defending champion Richard Petty and the other top Plymouth and Dodge drivers of the day, the

1965 season had been a disaster for track owners and fans alike. Yet history would repeat itself—sort of—in 1966, when Ford teams sat on the sidelines as the year began. The second boycott was again caused by an engine ban and again sidelined the defending champion. This time, though, it was Ford's overhead-cam 427-cubic-inch engine that was banned and 1965 titleholder Ned Jarrett on the sidelines.

Eventually a compromise of sorts was reached between France and one of Ford's top factory teams. Star racer Fred Lorenzen, a driver with movie star good looks and charm to burn, was slated to return the blue oval brand to action August 7 at Atlanta in a car owned and prepared by Johnson, who broke ranks with Ford, apparently due to concessions he received from France over how his car would be prepared.

The car in question, along with Smokey Yunick's black-and-gold Chevrolet Chevelle, which competed in the same race, was the most outrageous, bodacious, and flagrantly illegal car to ever compete in a NASCAR event. Dubbed the "Yellow Banana," Johnson's 1966 Ford Galaxie had its top chopped three to five inches—depending on whose estimate one believes—and its windshield was laid back at least 20 degrees. Its nose nearly touched the ground, and its rear quarter panels were swept upward to produce downforce, a modification that made the supposedly straight Galaxie sheet metal curve more like a banana.

Just how bogus was the banana? Thirty years later, *Speedworld* journalist Matt McLaughlin would say that the Yellow Banana looked about as much like a stock Ford Galaxie as his granny looked like Heather Locklear. In point of fact, it looked better suited to compete as an NHRA (National Hot Rod Association) funny car than it did as a NASCAR "stock car."

"They literally had to lift Lorenzen up and slide him into the driver's seat," remembers Bud Moore, who covered the race for the *Charlotte Observer*. "There was no way he could climb in it normally because the roof was slanted. And the front windshield was also sloped at an angle. The left side of the car was down about three inches lower than the right side of the car. Because Ford was struggling to stay in the sport, NASCAR basically turned their back on this deal and said, 'This is fine.'"

Not that Yunick's black-and-gold No. 13 Chevelle was any more legal, given that it was built to roughly 7/8 scale relative to its stock counterpart and carried an oversized engine, among a laundry list of infractions. Among the other "innovations" on Yunick's car that weekend were a built-in roof spoiler, offset frame, and removed drip rails on the roof.

Amazingly, both cars sailed through tech inspection, much to the outrage of Cotton Owens, who owned the Dodge that points leader David Pearson was driving that weekend. "The Chrysler guys went berserk when they saw the cars Johnson and Yunick slid through tech inspection," Moore said. "Cotton decided that one of the advantages of Lorenzen's car was that it was sitting so much lower than everybody else's. So what Cotton did, he fixed up Pearson's car where the whole car would literally drop about three inches. And NASCAR figured it out on Sunday morning, so they went to Cotton and said, 'OK, you cannot let Pearson use this device.'

"The four springs would compress, and the car would drop. Well, NASCAR said he couldn't use those springs. You've got to use regular springs. Well Cotton refused to do it, so he pulls the car out of the race. In that same race, Curtis Turner was driving for Smokey, who decided his engine was going to be about 20 cubic inches more than anybody else's. But the weird thing is, Turner is leading most of the race, and he blows up, so they never catch Smokey's car. Lorenzen crashes and Cotton pulled his car out. There was so much cheatin' going on that weekend, it was fun covering it, because every day it was a new deal."

One of France's most dramatic uses or misuses of power involved allowing two flagrantly illegal cars to compete to appease Detroit auto execs eager to get Ford and Chevrolet racing again as well as Atlanta track owners, who wanted all three automakers competing to revive attendance, which had sagged badly in 1965–66. The repercussions were profound. Pearson lost the 1966 NASCAR Grand National championship because he sat out the Atlanta race, due to Owens's disgust at perceived rules manipulation.

The Yellow Banana would never race again, because the factory Ford teams soon returned, the fans were appeased, and France had no reason to look the other way for the good of the sport. The Atlanta race in 1966 would forever represent the high-water mark—or low-water mark, depending on your point of view—for cheating, innovating, creative engineering, whatever one cares to call it. When the teams arrived at Daytona in 1967, NASCAR was waiting with its first body templates.

The teams had some new tricks of their own. Ford, which had a serious horsepower disadvantage, had been secretly using its wind tunnel in Michigan to smooth out the contours of its Fairlane race cars. "We didn't call it cheating, we called it 'competition tuning,'" said Ford engineer Charlie Gray, who oversaw the automaker's stock car efforts in the 1960s. "I guess some people claim I'm the reason why they have templates. We didn't have any horsepower. We had the 427-wedge engine, and we were running against the hemi Dodge. We had to find some way to run competitively. We used to go in and spend 24 hours at a time in the wind tunnel. Nobody knew that. Nobody knew about wind tunnels at that time. They [NASCAR] claimed that some of the things on our automobiles were a little bit different than stock. Well, we didn't think so. Anyhow, they [NASCAR] came with the templates at Daytona in 1967.

"In 1965 and '66, especially '66, the cars that ran at Daytona were very droop-snooped. They looked like anteaters. You couldn't run templates on those things. But in '67 we were into it pretty hot and heavy with our Fairlanes, so NASCAR came with the templates. For some reason our Fairlanes, in 1967 at Daytona, the rain gutters [along the roof] 'fell off' before they got to the racetrack. I can't figure how that happened. Lin Kuchler [of NASCAR] came to me and told me about it. When the next race came around, all the rain gutters were back on. That's just an example of something somebody found that worked. But things like that were usually corrected by the next race."

The 1967 Daytona 500 ultimately would be captured by Mario Andretti, but only because of a late-race engine failure in David Pearson's hot-rod Dodge, which had been carefully "engineered" by Cotton Owens to lower its center of gravity and dramatically improve handling.

"In 1967 (for the Daytona 500), I moved the floorboards up inside the car three inches, just pulled the top and all down around it and welded it back together," Owens said. "It no sooner hit off my trailer than everybody was under it. Richard Petty had his whole crew under it. I took the body of the car and dropped it over the chassis three inches lower than it would have been. Looking at it from the outside it looked like any other stock automobile. But if you got your measurement from the top to the floor you saw it. I called NASCAR about it before I built it, and they said anything was OK as long as what went under the car was in good workmanship. That was the ruling. We cut that thing up, lowered the roll bars, moved the floor up in it, and welded it back together. I took it as low as I could without it being too obvious. I still met the ground clearance requirements, but I got the roof of my car down. The advantage was getting the car lower through the air. It was the fastest thing there. Something happened with the engine with less than a hundred miles to go or we would have won."

*When Cale Yarborough (11) beat Richard Petty (43)
and Bobby Allison (12) in the 1973 National 500 at
Charlotte Motor Speedway, Allison threatened to sue
NASCAR, claiming he was beaten by two cars with
oversized engines. (Don Hunter)*

Chapter 4

If you don't cheat, you look like an idiot. If you do it and you don't get caught, you look like a hero. If you do it and get caught, you look like a dope. Put me in the category where I belong.

—Darrell Waltrip

The 1970s
Anything Goes

As the tumultuous 1960s came to an end, NASCAR was at a crossroads of sorts. The Big Three automakers scaled back their involvement in racing as they began to scale back their manufacturing of high-performance muscle cars for the street. The old phrase "win on Sunday, sell on Monday" seemed less relevant as Chevrolet, Ford, and Chrysler all phased out their respective 400-plus cubic-inch big-block engines in the early 1970s and starting building economy cars like the Vega and Pinto.

With less factory support to rely on, corporate sponsors entered the scene. R. J. Reynolds joined forces with NASCAR in 1971 to take over sponsorship of what had been known since the 1950s as the NASCAR Grand National series, renaming it the Winston Cup Series. Corporate America mainstays such as Coca-Cola, STP, and Gatorade became sponsors of race teams. Where a stock car once might have had its quarter panels festooned with the name of a local car dealership, now they became 170 mph billboards hawking beer or soft drinks. Teams started to look for sponsors to help foot the bills, and sponsors wanted to be associated with fast cars. And for some teams, the easiest way to run fast was to bend the rules—or break them altogether.

"The factories were getting out, so guys were trying to find ways to make more money by winning races," said Bob Moore. "That was when we first got sponsorships. So to help attract attention to themselves, they wanted to win. It's like anything else. The more visible you are when you go into somebody's office, the better chance you have of them saying, 'Oh yeah, we'll give you $50,000 or $20,000 or $10,000, whatever.' And also, when Richard [Petty] won the 27 races [in 1967], the other competitors got tired of Richard beating them to death. So they decided the only way to beat the boy was they had to cheat to beat him. So that was part of this equation that was going on back then. They were convinced he was cheating, they didn't know how he was cheating, but they figured the only way to beat him was to outcheat him."

Little did they know that Petty wasn't cheating, but he had found that putting as much weight as possible on the left side of the car would make it handle better. Petty and his teammates could actually adjust the weight balance of the car from inside the cockpit with a device called a weight jacker. It was a huge competitive advantage at the time, though not an illegal one.

"I've got pictures of Richard Petty getting in his car at a short track when he blew the engine in his car and got into Jim Paschal's car, which was owned by Petty," said Ford's Charlie Gray. "He was over a lap down. He was getting in his car and had a socket wrench in his firesuit, in the left-hand pocket.

Within 40 laps he was running faster than anybody. We all knew he was running a weight jacker."

"The left-side weight on the car [was] something that nobody was doing, and the rule book didn't address it because, in those days, they weighed the whole car, and the car was supposed to weigh 4,000 pounds," said Humpy Wheeler. "It didn't matter where the weight was."

As always, Junior Johnson was a force to be reckoned with, whether his cars were 100 percent legal or not. "If you wreck a car, you always try to build it back better. You'd keep adding little things and little ideas to it," Johnson explained. "Over a period of two or three years, first thing you know you've found something you like that really helps you. In the late 1960s, I had cars that were offset, motors moved back in them, wheels that were moved forward or backward depending on where I was running. Many, many things that I was doing were an advantage. Moving the wheels underneath the car to the left, widening the car out. There were many things that would help a car handle better."

Although not formally educated, Johnson figured out what the paid engineers knew about chassis setups. In general, the car would be fastest with its weight lower than higher. It would also be offset to the left as much as possible and back toward the center of the car rather than at the ends.

"In the early '70s [with Cale Yarborough driving] I did an Oldsmobile that I moved the wheels on, moved the motor back, moved everything to the left side. Moved the wheels further to the left side and to the front. It kept the front end down where it wouldn't lift up. It's a tremendous advantage to get the car down on the racetrack," Johnson said.

One of Johnson's favorite short-track enhancements was to start the race with trick tires and then change them on the first pit stop. "Junior, he was a master at self-defense," laughed Barry Dodson. "I know particularly at North Wilkesboro, when Cale would start the race, he'd be all over the racetrack until the first pit stop. They'd take those four tires off, and the rest of the day that car was a rocket. Little did people know those four tires had steel bands welded around them and they were poured with lead and they weighed a hundred pounds apiece. All of a sudden, he's 400 pounds light. They finally caught on to that when it took three crewmembers to get them over the wall. Junior always was a master at taking advantage of stuff like that." Eventually, NASCAR would decide to weigh cars both after the race and before.

"Talk about creative," said former crew chief Larry McReynolds. "It was against the rules because they were 80 or 100 pounds light [per tire], but you think about the places where they always kicked butt—North Wilkesboro, Martinsville, the road courses, Richmond—that's places where that was so important. And it was done pretty regular. NASCAR didn't weigh cars after the races then. They do now."

Johnson was pretty sharp on the aerodynamic front as well. "If you remember his race cars, they always had pretty extravagant paint schemes," said McReynolds. "It wasn't because Junior thought that was pretty. Paint schemes can cover up a lot of stuff. You can put several different colors and maybe some pinstriping, where if you painted it solid if would have a totally different look. Most of Junior's cars had some pretty creative paint schemes to them, because he was hiding aero stuff. If he had something that was supposed to have a sharp edge but a radius was a lot better, he put in a paint line or maybe a pinstripe. It gives it that edge look but it's a radius the whole time."

"Junior Johnson was a stand-on-the-gas, go-for-it kind of racer. He was a good racer," said Robert Yates, who worked for Johnson in the 1970s. "He didn't care about something being pretty as much as he wanted it effective. It was quite a university there. I learned a lot about how to build engines. If you had some idea about something new or different, he would really wake up to it. 'Let's do it.' I'd say, 'I don't know, it might not be legal.' He'd say, 'That's all right.' He was the type of guy that you sort of wanted to be on his side if there was going to be a fight. His theory was let's design something and design it wrong, but be able [to make it legal] in seconds. I probably have some of his mix in me. He's one of my big heroes. He would be aggressive. He wasn't a right-by-the-book kind of person. His adrenaline pumped when he was fudging things. That was racing back then, doing things differently. There just weren't enough policemen. There were too many of us trying to beat the system."

In doctoring his cars, Johnson ran into the same problem Yunick had 10 or 15 years earlier. "I had people who worked for me who would talk, couldn't keep their mouth shut," Johnson said. "Couldn't keep things a secret very long. But I could go back late at night and do things myself, and nobody would know anything about it. When I did that, I could get by with a lot of stuff. And it wasn't that you were cheating. There weren't a lot of rules. It was just that you found a way to beat everybody because you had done enough homework to be where you were at."

One place where Johnson and many other teams did their homework was on the weigh-in scales. Getting a light car through became a high art.

"We decided at Martinsville to run light was really a good deal. We figured out a way to beat the scales. In fact, we beat the scales a lot of places," said Yates. "Just knew how to drive the car on it right. You could beat the scales at every racetrack, I believe, except Charlotte. I even figured out a way of beating the Charlotte scales by putting a piece of tape under the left rear tire and timing it and turning my steering wheel a little bit so we could pitch the weight to the right side. I could beat every scale just a little bit just knowing how to drive the car on there. Finally, NASCAR put separate scales out for each of the four wheels to eliminate that."

"We used to have the old grain scales that we'd roll the cars across," Dodson recalled. " We didn't have the digital stuff you have today. If you were one of the last cars to be weighed, you could take a little magnet and hang it on the bottom of that car and change the reading on the scale by a hundred pounds."

"When they ran them across the scales and weighed each wheel, we always had somebody standing around with their arm propped on the car or something like that," said Bud Moore. "You could get by fairly good on a lot of stuff. We were supposed to weigh back then probably 3,700 pounds. We were usually a hundred pounds light."

Perhaps the most clever way to beat the weight limit was discovered by a young mechanic named Gary Nelson, who worked with Darrell Waltrip at DiGard Racing in the late 1970s.

Nelson came up with a variation on the old drop-the-buckshot trick that racer Jack Smith said he first saw in the early 1960s. Nelson's execution was brilliant in its simplicity: The buckshot was dumped into the frame through a hole under the battery and released from the jack plate on the frame rails. So whenever NASCAR inspectors went to look under Waltrip's car, the very first thing they did was put a jack under the side of the car and lift it up, which covered up the spring-loaded release plate. When he'd release the buckshot, Waltrip often would get on the team's radio and announce, "Bombs away!" Instantly, the car was 75 to 300 pounds lighter, depending on how much buckshot had been put in to begin with.

But the teams all saved their best tricks for the Daytona 500, then as now the most important race of the year. Daytona drew the most attention and sponsor interest, got the most exposure, and paid extremely well. But in those days, the annual January testing at the 2.5-mile superspeedway was not closely supervised by NASCAR, and cars didn't have to test in legal trim. If a team was looking for a sponsor prior to Daytona and wanted to generate some buzz, all it had to do was bolt in a 500-cubic-inch motor for a January test session and run some blisteringly fast lap times. All of a sudden the word would get around about how fast it was running. There was no better or quicker way to attract a sponsor's dollars.

And sometimes the big engines found their way into real races. In the 1973 National 500 at Charlotte Motor Speedway, tensions were high among competitors, who felt that cheating had reached epidemic proportions. Even those doing the cheating were concerned. During a practice session three days after qualifying, pole-winner Charlie Glotzbach was found to have an illegal carburetor plate in his Hoss Ellington–owned Chevrolet. NASCAR disqualified his pole-winning time, forcing him to requalify. Ellington swore the offending part was used only in practice, not qualifying, prompting journalist Benny Phillips to note that "The penalty of disqualifying Glotzbach is like putting someone in jail on Saturday for being drunk on Wednesday."

After the race, the cars of race winner Cale Yarborough, who drove for Junior Johnson at the time, runner-up Richard Petty, and third-place finisher Bobby Allison all had their engines torn down. Some 25 hours after the race was over, Yarborough was declared the winner, even though there were allegations that the first- and second-place cars were running oversized engines.

"Prior to the inspection Allison claimed he saw crew members from Petty's crew run over and, using rags to hide what they were up to, remove something from the engine compartment, while a nearby NASCAR official conveniently turned his back," recalled Matt McLaughlin of the Web site SpeedFx. "Allison's car passed quickly, but there was obviously something up in the inspection garage, as the post-race inspection dragged on six hours. Rumors were circulating [that] Petty's engine was a little oversized and Yarborough's was way out of line."

According to accounts from NASCAR journalist and historian Greg Fielden, track promoter Richard Howard blew his cool over the lengthy inspection process. "They give you a stamp of approval at race time and six hours later can't give you a winner," Fielden quoted Howard as saying. "I've been paying NASCAR inspectors to be here all week and ensure that the cars are legal. Now they tell me they might not have done their job and some illegal cars may have gotten by them. If so, what have I been spending my money for? If they rule against the order of finish that the fans saw on Sunday, I'm going to court. By letting the cars start, the NASCAR inspectors said that they were OK. Now they are reneging. I'm not bluffing about this. I'm sick and tired of seeing stuff like this be allowed to happen, possibly leading to the ruin of a great sport."

Amazingly, NASCAR made an announcement the next day that the Yarborough-Petty-Allison finishing order would remain one-two-three because its post-race inspection was "inadequate" to determine the cubic inches of the cars involved. "The decision to let the results stand was made following a meeting of NASCAR officials after reviewing information that showed in a post-race inspection the procedure used to check all of the engine sizes in the previous race inspection proved inadequate," the sanctioning body said in a prepared statement. "Since the purpose of the pre-race inspection is to determine that the cars in competition conform to the rules prior to the actual running of the race and that this procedure was in effect for the Charlotte race, the results are official."

Outraged, Allison threatened to sue, claiming NASCAR officials had told him Petty's engine was a little oversized, while Johnson's was "a whopper." On October 11, Allison announced his plans to pursue legal action. "If you use the standards utilized by NASCAR, we ought to give [former vice president and convicted felon] Spiro Agnew his job back," Fielden reported Allison as saying. "If you get caught cheating, it doesn't seem to matter in NASCAR's eyes. I'm just one of 38 guys who got cheated. It was just a case of NASCAR having to discipline the little guys because they don't have enough guts to do what's right with the big guys."

He dropped the idea after a lengthy closed-door meeting with NASCAR President Bill France Jr. on October 15. "I have received satisfactory restitution, and you can read that any way you want" was Allison's only comment, though it was widely rumored that France had used his legendary powers of persuasion to calm the driver down. In fact, the rumor—never proven or disproven—was that France had given Allison a hefty check to settle the issue, perhaps as much as $50,000. Neither man would ever speak of the incident publicly again.

Twenty-eight years later, Robert Yates, who built the engine for Cale Yarborough's Charlotte-winning car, confirmed that it was way oversized, but insisted that those found in the competitors' engine bays were, too.

"I just built a big one," Yates said. "There were so many ways of beating the system. Finally, I just got great big [with engine displacement]. We had 500-cubic-inch motors. I sent one to Martinsville, and [crew chief] Herb Nab called me back at the shop and said, 'Man, this thing is so bad it's laying two streaks of rubber all the way down the straightaway.' It was just a hog motor. We went to North Wilkesboro the next week and then to Charlotte, and by that time NASCAR knew that something was going on. So they were going to pull the cylinder heads off everybody. We won the race. We were there all night. They pulled the heads off and started trying to measure the bore and stroke. They didn't really have the equipment to do it. Eight different people checked our engine and came up with eight different sizes. They finally let us out at midnight. So what? Everybody else had big motors. From that day forward they started pulling heads off, that made you look around and say this is all fair now. I sort of was happy that it all got [more heavily policed by NASCAR]."

While it was Allison who had raised a stink at Charlotte that year, the proverbial shoe would be on the other foot a year later, when Allison ran afoul of NASCAR inspectors. At Ontario, California, Allison won the final race of the season, only to have his car caught with illegal roller tappets, instead of the solid ones mandated by NASCAR. The roller tappets, which fit between the camshaft and pushrods have less friction than solid lifters and thus produce more horsepower.

"He almost got away with it," former NASCAR Winston Cup Director Dick Beaty said in a 1988 interview with *NASCAR Winston Cup Scene*'s Deb Williams. "I told one of the crewmen to hand me one of the tappets. At first, they pretended like they couldn't get if off. I told him he was going to take it apart if we had to cut it. Finally, they got one out. The one he handed me was as cold as ice. He had a rag in his hand and it had a flat tappet in it. When he pulled the roller tappet out of the car, he kept it in his rag and handed me the flat one. Now, there's no way a tappet that's just come out of a car that's run 500 miles is going to be cold. I grabbed the rag that was in his hand and sure enough, there was the roller tappet. If he had taken that [flat] tappet and heated it, he would have gotten away with it."

But illegal engine modifications weren't the only way enterprising teams tried to skirt the rules. In an effort to equalize competition among the various makes and hold speeds as well, NASCAR stepped up its use of restrictor plates. The way a restrictor plate works is very simple: It is a machined flat aluminum plate that fits between the carburetor and intake manifold and uses small-diameter openings to limit the amount of fuel-air mixture that flows from the carburetor into the engine, drastically reducing horsepower. Although NASCAR has used a variety of different sizes and configurations of restrictor plates over the years, in the contemporary motors used today at superspeedways, they cut horsepower from about 780 to 400.

From the onset of their use, however, restrictor plates have been a source of almost infinite temptation for engine builders and crew chiefs who want to tamper with the devices. During the running of the 1973 Winston 500 at Talladega, Marty Robbins, a country and western singer and part-time stock-car racer, finished 18th and turned race laps 15 mph faster than his qualifying speed, raising some eyebrows in the garage.

"Marty loved to race for a hobby. He didn't do it for money," recalled Dick Thompson of the late singer. "He went to Talladega and he was running like a bandit, but what they had done, is they had fiddled with his restrictor plate. He won rookie of the race and everything, but he went to NASCAR and he told 'em, 'I'm not running legal, I just wanted to get out there one time and race with 'em.' Nobody would hold that against Marty 'cause he was such a great guy."

"When they first started putting the plates on the cars, when I drove for Holman-Moody, old Jake [Elder] had a big restrictor plate taped up under the fan cover," recalled David Pearson of the early 1970s. "Back then NASCAR would hand you the plate and you'd turn around and put it on. Old Jake just turned right around and stuck the one NASCAR gave him up under the fan cover and pulled the other one out and put it on the car. Looking at it, you couldn't tell the difference. You can take a knife and go around those holes in the restrictor plate, open them up just a little and pick up 10 horsepower. We run the 125-milers [Daytona 500 qualifying races] that way. NASCAR came over and said they wanted to see it. All they wanted to do was look down in the carburetor and see that the plate was still on it. Jake got mad and jerked the seal off. They said, well since you broke the seal just go ahead and take the carburetor off. If he hadn't done that we would have gotten away with it. But all I was doing was looking in my mirror and driving just fast enough to stay in front of them. I could have run a lot faster, but you've got to use your head when you're doing something like that. But we got caught. There has been a lot of cheating going on with the plate. I would say there still are people cheating with it someway, somehow."

Another master manipulator of the restrictor plate was former car owner Hoss Ellington, who campaigned cars for

Sterling Marlin and the late Tim Richmond, as well as Charlie Glotzbach's disqualified 1973 Charlotte car, among others. His most famous car was the one Donnie Allison drove in 1979, when he crashed with Cale Yarborough going for the win on the last lap of the Daytona 500.

"When the carburetor plate first came out, Hoss had a device," said Bob Moore. "The restrictor plate was set in there. Hoss developed a pull device, and it would actually slide the hole completely open. It was incredible. It was so intricately machined it was almost invisible to the human eye. And he actually got away with it for a couple of races before they found it. Hoss was a little bit strange in that he enjoyed getting caught. Then he'd make a big uproar and cause a big stink. Unlike, say, Junior [Johnson] and a few others, whose whole idea was never to get caught, if Hoss got away with it, fine. If he didn't get away with it, fine."

In 1986, Marlin's Ellington-owned Chevrolet Monte Carlo was penalized for having an illegal fuel cooling system prior to the Firecracker 400 at Daytona in July. Marlin's car had a hidden padded metal box filled with dry ice and a spiraled fuel line that ran through it. The dry ice cooled the fuel, making it more dense, so it would generate additional horsepower under combustion.

Pearson, who drove briefly for Ellington, said the outspoken owner loved the conspiracy aspect of cheating but was not mechanically inclined himself. "Hoss never did know what to do," Pearson said. "[Engine builder] Runt [Pittman] was the main one on that car. He's the one who did all the cheating and stuff. I know one time when I drove his car, Runt took

a grease fitting and screwed a hole for it in the intake manifold. Hoss couldn't stand it. He wanted to know what that
grease fitting was for. Runt told him, 'Don't worry, it's
something that's going to help it.' Hoss couldn't wait to tell
people about it. But Runt was just messing around with him.
It didn't really do anything."

For NASCAR Winston Cup teams in the 1970s, though,
the clear performance booster of choice was nitrous oxide,
or NO_2. Known as laughing gas and used for years as a med-
ical sedative, nitrous oxide injected into an internal
combustion engine generates a tremendous horsepower
boost—upwards of 100 horsepower over a short period. In
the mid-1970s, many NASCAR Winston Cup teams hid
nitrous oxide canisters in the bodies and frames of their cars.
Though a tank might last long enough for only 30 to 40 seconds, used at the right time, it could mean the difference
between winning and losing.

Nitrous oxide was especially popular during qualifying,
when it could mean the difference between sitting on the pole
and missing the race entirely. The biggest nitrous oxide scan-
dal occurred in 1976, at the biggest race of the season, the
Daytona 500. Pole-sitter A. J. Foyt and second-qualifier
Darrell Waltrip both had their times disallowed after nitrous
oxide was found in their respective cars. During the same race,
Dave Marcis's qualifying time was also disallowed because he
was caught with a movable air deflector in his car, a device that
could reduce drag and make his car faster.

Foyt and NASCAR President Bill France Jr., who had succeeded his father as NASCAR's leader in 1972, nearly came to blows at Daytona back then, with the volatile Texan proclaiming he hadn't used nitrous oxide. Twenty-five years later, prior to the running of the 2001 Daytona 500, Foyt still maintained he didn't use the performance-enhancing substance. "He's not talking to anybody about it, but if he was, he'd tell you the same thing he did back then: He didn't do it," said team spokesman Michael Rompf.

The ever-effusive Waltrip, however, admitted his team had nitrous in the car. "If you don't cheat, you look like an idiot. If you do it and you don't get caught, you look like a hero. If you do it and get caught, you look like a dope. Put me in the category where I belong," he said at the time.

Prior to the 2000 running of the Brickyard 400, Waltrip spilled the whole story. "We went to Daytona and [crew chief] Mario Rossi took what we called the wedge bar and made that into a cylinder and packed it full of nitrous," he told reporters Robin Miller and Curt Cavin of the *Indianapolis Star*. But NASCAR officials became suspicious of Foyt and Waltrip when their practice times were a second per lap slower than their qualifying speeds.

"So here comes NASCAR. They took my car into the inspection room and had people crawl all over it. We were trying not to laugh, but it was hard because they were hanging on that bar with the nitrous," Waltrip said. "Finally, Bill France Sr. and Bill Gazaway came over and said if we didn't tell them where the nitrous was, they were going to go get the saw and cut every bar on the car out. Rossi got nervous they might cut into something and blow themselves up, so he told them where it was."

The fears of a nitrous oxide tank exploding were not unwarranted, either. "In the nitrous oxide days, when everybody was doing it, I saw an oil tank blow apart down at Darlington one day on a race car, because the nitrous oxide went off in the car," said car owner Richard Childress.

"The funniest one of those was G. C. Spencer at Talladega, because he had it in his car and it went off in the garage area. There was this loud hissing sound," said historian Bob Latford. "Another time, D. K. Ulrich, one of the independents, had a cylinder hidden in the front cross-member. And when he crashed, it was stripped away from the car."

Car owner Bud Moore said nitrous oxide was fairly common in the 1970s. "Several people got caught using it. They had it hidden all around. All you had to do was turn a little valve and shoot it into the air cleaner," he said. "It'd raise the horsepower, 30 or 40 more, just like that. You run your first lap, got the speed up, then put that boost to it. Most of them had the bottle inside the seat. Tube ran out the seat bar, worked its way around, and got its way into the air cleaner. It was hard to detect."

Although he denied using nitrous, Foyt did admit to Miller and Cavin that he wasn't 100 percent legal all the time in the 1970s. "The biggest thing you could get away with was messing with the body of the car," he said. "Cale [Yarborough] and I had Oldsmobiles that we narrowed, but somebody blew the whistle on us and NASCAR wouldn't even let us unload them off the trailer."

"My job is to drive the car. It is my brother,s [Maurice] job to work on the engines. It,s his decision as to what to put in the car, not mine. As for the wrong tires, it was a mistake by the crew. I accept the NASCAR penalty." —Richard Petty

Chapter 5

I said, "Well, you cheating son of a bitch. I can see getting by with 10 or 20 pounds light, but 220?" He said, "Well, if you're going to cheat, you might as well cheat."

—Bud Moore

The 1980s
Playing Favorites

One of the biggest cheating scandals in NASCAR's history remains to this day one of the most enigmatic. It occurred October 9, 1983, at the Miller High Life 500 at Charlotte Motor Speedway. In that race, Richard Petty made a late charge to put his Petty Enterprises Pontiac into victory lane, finishing three seconds ahead of Darrell Waltrip's Junior Johnson–owned Chevrolet.

The win, the 198th of Petty's illustrious career, seemed normal enough at first. On the last round of pit stops, which occurred on lap 292 of the 334-lap race, Petty came out second behind Waltrip. Twenty laps later, he went by Waltrip and never looked back, cruising to an easy victory, one that raised some eyebrows in the Johnson camp. "Petty came by pretty quick," Waltrip said after the race. "It's funny how your perspective is. Nothing happened to us. It's just that he picked up. He ran a lot better than us at the end. We didn't slow down."

But there was nothing funny about what occurred during the routine post-race teardown, when NASCAR inspectors made two shocking discoveries: First, Petty's team had put left-side tires on the right side during the team's final pit stop, a clear violation of rules and a tremendous traction advantage. NASCAR mandates different rubber compound for each side of Winston Cup cars, with the harder, more durable tires on the left side, where most of the load is at speed. Running softer left-side tires on the right gives a car better traction for a short time, though they will wear out quicker than the harder tires mandated by the rule book.

The second offense was even more remarkable and flagrant: The engine in Petty's car measured 381.983 cubic inches, nearly 24 cubic inches over the allowable maximum of 358 cubic inches.

Neither one of these violations could be ignored or dismissed as "pushing the gray area" or "looking for a competitive advantage." This was flagrant cheating, pure and simple, and it was committed by a family-owned team whose driver was both the most winning in the sport's history and the most popular. This was a black eye that NASCAR didn't need, a blow to its squeaky clean image just as the sport was starting to break out of its rural, Southern roots and gain national attention.

The rules infractions were announced some four hours after the race ended by then NASCAR Competition Director Bill Gazaway. Prior to the announcement, Petty said only that something had happened in tech inspection, but he didn't know what. By the time Gazaway made his disclosure, Petty was long gone, headed back to his home in Level Cross, North Carolina, as was Johnson, who lived about an hour away in Wilkes County.

Petty was allowed to keep the victory, but was docked 104 Winston Cup points and fined $35,000, the largest penalty ever levied by NASCAR up to that point. The 104-point penalty kept Petty in fourth place in the championship race, leading Harry Gant by the same margin he had going into the race.

Years earlier, Big Bill France had made a basic policy decision. According to France, fans who came to a race had to know whom the winner was when they left. France and his son Bill Jr. had the power to deal with cheaters through fines, suspensions, or any other way they deemed fit, and their rules and methods could and did change any time, but by God the guy who crossed the finish line first was declared the winner and that was that.

Needless to say, not everyone agreed with that logic; in fact, one could make a compelling case that it encouraged cheating rather than discouraged it. But that's the way the Frances ran things and still do. So Petty's victory stood, and both a cash fine and a points penalty were levied.

In a prepared statement issued the following day, Petty denied knowledge of the infractions. "My job is to drive the car," Petty said October 10 in a prepared statement. "It is my brother's [Maurice] job to work on the engines. It's his decision as to what to put in the car, not mine. As for the wrong tires, it was a mistake by the crew. I accept the NASCAR penalty." Few others did, however.

Waltrip and his car owner Johnson both claimed they were outraged by the decision, especially given that they were seeking a third straight championship and were locked in a tight points battle with Bobby Allison. Johnson threatened to sue, claiming the massively oversized engine was the "difference between first-degree murder and manslaughter."

"NASCAR is crookeder than what Petty has done," Johnson told *NASCAR Winston Cup Scene* reporter Jack Flowers. "In the future, the credibility of the sport will be questioned because of the decision." He also wasn't happy with Petty for placing the blame on his brother Maurice. "It's his operation; he's the driver, and he's responsible for what happens. I always thought more of Richard Petty than he'd accept a decision like that. To let racing take a blow like it's taking, if he's wrong and he knows he's wrong, he should not accept something that will hurt the sport like this will hurt it down the road," said the man who raced the Yellow Banana in 1966 and had run a 500-cubic-inch engine a decade earlier at Charlotte.

"I'm not mad at Richard, but somebody has failed to do his job in handling this," added Waltrip. "There is no question I'm the winner."

"I'm sure Petty's not the first driver who won a race and was caught cheating, but it certainly doesn't seem fair to allow him the victory when there were others out there racing who didn't have bigger engines and left-side tires on the wrong side," Terry Labonte told Flowers, who also drew an angry reaction from Robert Harrington, crew chief for J. D. Stacy's team.

"When they caught us at Darlington with a hot engine which measured 358.2 cubic inches, during the time given us for a cool-down period Gazaway came up to me and told me if the engine was illegal we could lose everything," Harrington said. "Now Petty gets caught with an engine that's so big you could freeze it and it would still be illegal. They give him the victory and take away money and the margin he gained in the points. NASCAR threatens a little guy like me who needs every crumb he can get and it slaps Petty on the wrist. I think the rule should fit a Richard Petty the same way it does a Ronnie Thomas."

Reporter Bob Moore said that the Charlotte race was the climax to a long-simmering battle over who was and who wasn't cheating. "Allison had been complaining all year long that Petty and Junior were illegal and NASCAR had not been able to find it," said Moore. "The mistake that was made by the Pettys was that the engine was illegal, and when they put left sides on the right side, it was so obvious what they were doing, In most cases, left-side tires were smaller than right sides. So NASCAR was more or less forced to say, 'Whoa, wait a minute.'

"Junior, knowing what was going on, took his race car home," Moore continued. "He was never inspected. As soon as the race was over with—Darrell finished second—they loaded the car up. Darrell literally came off the racetrack, and they had the back gate of the transporter open. Because Junior knew what was going to happen with the No. 43 car [Petty's], the No. 11 car [Waltrip's] was in the hauler. The 11 hauler was fighting its way through fans. It was past midnight when they came and told us [Petty's] car was illegal. By the time NASCAR figured out what was going on, the 11 car was long gone." In fact, Petty's car was the only one inspected after the race. NASCAR had planned to inspect Waltrip's car, but never got the chance.

In the past, other teams had used big engines, as Yates admitted. During inspection, engine displacement is calculated simply by filling one of an engine's eight cylinders with a volume of liquid, measuring how many cubic inches of liquid it held and multiplying that number by eight. Of course, a lot of guys found creative ways to get around the rules.

"Getting by with an oversized engine, you could put something like a cigarette filter or paraffin in the cylinder, so when they check it for displacement, it measures right," said NASCAR historian Bob Latford. "But once it gets hot and runs, the paraffin would melt or the filter would blow out, so you'd have that empty space to compress and get a higher compression ratio and turn faster." And if you somehow found out ahead of time which of the eight cylinders would be measured, you could build an engine with one cylinder the legal size and seven dramatically oversized, either with a cylinder that had an extra-wide circumference, a dimension known as bore, or a piston that traveled a longer distance up and down in the cylinder, which is called stroke. Potentially, such an arrangement could cause some internal vibration and balance issues, but a smart engine builder might be able to minimize such problems.

Ironically, the one driver who came to Petty's defense was Bobby Allison, who had in his employ a young and creative crew chief named Gary Nelson. "In my opinion, Petty has shot straighter than anyone over the years. Anyone but me, that is," Allison said. "I don't think we can fully criticize Petty if the second-place car wasn't checked, too. And as far back in the field as necessary, for that matter."

Allison also said the winning car should be torn down and inspected by the second- and third-place finishers. "I still think the mechanics of those cars should do the checking," Allison said. "The NASCAR guys are very dedicated. But if their $30,000- to $40,000-a-year men have to match wits with $100,000-a-year men, they are going to let some things get by them.

"If the second- and third-place men had looked at Petty's car," Allison continued, "this would never have come up. I think it's sad that it had to happen at all, and if I knew they were going to look at the engine in my car, we'd make darn sure that it would never measure over 357.999 cubic inches, or whatever."

Allison, of course, was no stranger to controversy, either, or cars with questionable features and preparation. In 1982, the rear bumper of Allison's DiGard-owned, Gary Nelson–wrenched car fell off during the Daytona 500 after Allison's car received a slight tap from behind early in the race— an almost inconceivable scenario given the bulletproof construction of Winston Cup cars. But Allison's Buick was both lightened and improved aerodynamically once the bumper fell off, and he drove on to an eyebrow-raising victory.

Was the bumper designed to fall off? "There were accusations," Nelson told *Miami Herald* reporter Gary Long in 2000. "That was definitely an accident. But circumstances piled up to where I couldn't defend myself. So I've tried to remain quiet on that one."

Robert Yates, who worked as an engine builder at DiGard while Allison was driving, made it equally clear in his own way that the team was not above bending the rules in the early 1980s. "When I was at DiGard we had more blue bottles than wrenches," Yates said of the wide variety of perform-ance-enhancing—and almost certainly illegal—products used in the team's shops.

Perhaps the goings-on at DiGard and Johnson's teams led Allison to defend Petty. Although he never publicly said why he built the monster motor, Maurice Petty hinted that it was because he was tired of being beaten by teams that he felt certain were cheating. "I did it," he said shortly after that Charlotte race. "And I'm not so sure I wouldn't do it again under similar circumstances. What I don't like is people calling my brother Richard the cheater. I'm the one who cheated. Not him."

Nearly 20 years after the event, this much is certain: The 1980s represented the period when there was the greatest discrepancy between the sophistication of race teams and the resources of NASCAR and its inspection process. This was a time of tremendous lawlessness in racing, as teams began to make the transition from shade-tree mechanics to high-tech engineers complete with computers, wind tunnels, and a host of other tools. NASCAR would take years to catch up.

NASCAR's chief inspector at the time was Dick Beaty, who assumed the post of Winston Cup Director in May 1980, three months after he retired as the assistant manager of Charlotte/Douglas [North Carolina] International Airport. In 13 years as Winston Cup director, Beaty managed to institute many important changes in the sport, systematically organizing where teams parked their haulers in the garage, making inspections more methodical, and mandating the use of spotters on race day to help drivers avoid wrecks. He also made crew chiefs the official spokesmen for race teams. If a dispute broke out, it was the crew chief, and the crew chief only, who was allowed to speak to Beaty or NASCAR inspectors.

Beaty had the reputation of being a tough guy and an excellent organizer, but sometimes rules seemed to be made up as Beaty went along or were broken altogether.

One of the most brilliant minds to butt heads with Beaty was DiGard's Nelson. In July 1985, Greg Sacks stunned the NASCAR community by scoring his only career Winston Cup victory at the Firecracker 400 at Daytona. In that race, Sacks drove an unsponsored DiGard "research and development" car that featured a number of "experimental" parts. Like Junior Johnson's "Yellow Banana," Sacks's Chevrolet wasn't illegal when it ran but subsequently was banned. To this day, Nelson won't talk about the race, the car itself, or the unlikely victory, but few people believe that Sacks's car was 100 percent legal.

"Gary's cars always got good fuel mileage. *Really* good fuel mileage," said one former rival crew chief, strongly hinting that Nelson routinely figured out how to get more than 22 gallons of fuel into the car.

Nelson even admitted how his cars could go so far on a tank of gas: Ricky Rudd's 1981 DiGard car had an extra tank hidden in the frame. "It was directly over the rear end housing in a double panel," Nelson said in a 1998 interview with *NASCAR Winston Cup Scene*'s Steve Waid. "It was the full width of the frame. It was in a safer place than the legal 22-gallon tank and had its own separate [fuel pump] system. But

Above: When NASCAR raced at hardscrabble dirt tracks like Asheville-Weaverville (N.C.) in 1957, the competitors were supposed to be driving true stock cars. But already racers were "experimenting" with tires, chassis, engines, and bodywork to see where they could gain an advantage. (Don Hunter) Below: In two short years, Karl Kiekhaefer (left) established a winning percentage that no other stock-car team has come close to matching. In the process, he became vilified by fans and competitors and a constant target of NASCAR president Bill France's increasingly tough inspections. (Don Hunter)

Smokey Yunick was a true maverick and a constant thorn in France's side because *his outspoken nature and the host of tricks he pioneered, including a flywheel-drive* *supercharger and a two-inch-diameter fuel line that was 11 feet long and held an e*

Clockwise from top: When Curtis Turner started from the pole position in Yunick's Chevrolet Chevelle at Atlanta in 1966, the back of the roof was subtly swept upward to serve as a spoiler and produce downforce. The body was also offset to improve weight distribution./Junior Johnson clashed with NASCAR inspectors many times during his career as a driver and later, a team owner. Johnson and his crew competed with offset-wheelbase cars, engines that were oversized and relocated for better weight distribution, and modified bodywork to enhance aerodynamics./When Fred Lorenzen drove Junior Johnson's Ford Galaxie at Atlanta in 1966, it was immediately dubbed the "Yellow Banana" because the nose had been lowered, the rear sheet metal upswept, the roof channeled, and the angles of the front and rear bumpers moved. Despite howls of protest from other competitors about the obvious alterations, France let the car through inspection and into the race.
(Don Hunter)

Left: *NASCAR chief inspector Bill Gazaway (left) holds up an illegally modified carburetor restrictor plate removed from a Winston Cup car owned by Hoss Ellington (right). The center section of the plate slid out, greatly increasing horsepower. Charlie Glotzbach's pole-winning time at Charlotte in 1973 in an Ellington-owned Chevrolet was disqualified when the plate was discovered. (Don Hunter)* **Right:** *In the mid-1970s, one of NASCAR's biggest challenges was uncovering tanks of nitrous oxide, which crews hid in frame rails, under seats and dashboards, and anywhere else they could find. Nitrous oxide, or N_2O, provided brief boosts of 50 to 100 extra horsepower for a few seconds at a time. (Don Hunter)*

Right: *Gazaway shows off oversized fuel tanks confiscated from race teams. Squeezing an extra gallon or two of gas into the fuel system can means the difference between winning and losing, which is why teams through the years have gone to elaborate measures to increase fuel capacity and hide it from NASCAR. (Don Hunter)*

Left: Without the help of the draft or caution periods, Bill Elliott made up two laps under green-flag conditions at Talladega in 1985 to score one of NASCAR's most improbable victories. Now Ford's former lead aerodynamic engineer has suggested that the body on Elliott's Ford may have been narrower and lower than other Fords in the race. (Don Hunter)

Opposite: Bill Elliott's Ford Thunderbird passed NASCAR inspection at Talladega in 1985 and was declared legal. But Elliott's victory raised such eyebrows among competitors that his car was aggressively torn down after subsequent victories, which Elliott claimed wore the team down and cost him the championship. (Don Hunter)

Above: NASCAR officials prepare to hand out a restrictor plate at Talladega in April 1995. (Mike Horne)
Left: Racing legend A.J. Foyt (left) talks with Norris Friel, who was NASCAR's chief inspector in the mid-1960s. In 1976, Foyt and NASCAR president Bill France Jr. nearly came to blows at Daytona after Foyt's car was allegedly found with a tank of nitrous oxide. (Don Hunter)

Left: Jeff Gordon's victory in the 1997 Winston was accomplished with a car called "T-Rex," which had a purpose-built chassis designed to optimize performance over short distances, such as the final 10-lap segment that determines the winner of The Winston. (Mike Horne)

Above: *Jimmy Spencer shocked the Winston Cup community in 1994 when he won back-to-back restrictor-plate races at Daytona and Talladega while driving for Junior Johnson. They were the only two wins of his career. (Sam Sharpe)*

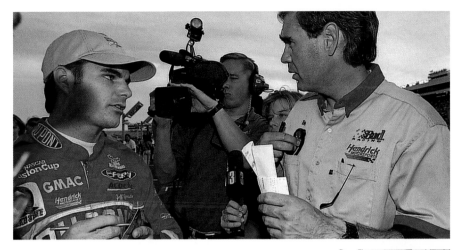

Above: Gordon's crew chief, Ray Evernham, outwitted competitors and the media alike by publicly complaining that NASCAR's banishment of his radical T-Rex chassis design would set the team back more than a year in development. In truth, Evernham never intended to race the T-Rex anywhere but in The Winston. (Tom Copeland)

Right: Wind-cheating low-drag decklids, like these seized at Talladega in October 1997 from the cars of Jeff Burton and Ernie Irvan, are the type of body parts that NASCAR inspectors frequently check at superspeedway races. (Mike Horne)

Left: After NASCAR inspectors ordered the rear fascia removed on Dale Earnhardt's Chevrolet at Talladega in April 2000, the team replaced it with a part that car owner Richard Childress later said was identical to the one removed. (Sam Sharpe)

NASCAR and Goodyear officials tightly regulate when tires are distributed over the course of a race weekend to help ensure that teams don't have the opportunity to try anything illegal, such as applying chemicals to the rubber to help improve traction. (Sam Sharpe)

Right: Prior to the 2001 Gatorade Twin 125 qualifying race, which determined the grid for the Daytona 500, a NASCAR inspector measures the precise angle of a rear spoiler to make sure it conforms to the rules. *(Sam Sharpe)*

Below: Jeff Gordon's victory in the CMT 300 at New Hampshire International Speedway in 1998 set off the controversy known as "Tiregate." Rival team owner Jack Roush alleged that Gordon and crew chief Ray Evernham used an illegal chemical additive to enhance the performance of their tires. NASCAR's lengthy investigation found nothing. *(Sam Sharpe)*

Left: To cut down on the potential for cheating on ride height, NASCAR standardized the rear shock absorbers used at Talladega, locked them up under guard, and randomly passed them out to teams immediately prior to practice, qualifying, and the race. *(DBP photo)*

Above: *NASCAR also measures wheelbase of the cars on both sides, here checking Bill Elliott's Dodge at Richmond International Raceway in 2001. (David A. Dalesandro)*

Right: One of the ways NASCAR has attempted to reduce cheating in recent years is to increase the number and scope of dimensions it measures. At Rockingham in 2000, an official measures the Wood Brothers—owned Ford of Elliott Sadler to make sure the specifications in the front end are correct. *(Sam Sharpe)*

Above: NASCAR uses nearly 30 templates to measure body dimensions down to fractions of an inch. In the early 1990s, NASCAR used only about a dozen templates, but gradually added more later in the decade. *(Sam Sharpe)*

Right: The relationship of the tires to the bodywork and wheel opening is checked on Mark Martin's Ford at Richmond in 2001. *(David A. Dalesandro)*

Left: Thanks to a precision gauge, NASCAR inspectors can determine instantly if a Winston Cup car meets minimum height requirements. (David A. Dalesandro)

Above: Dale Jarrett's car gets checked for height before the 2002 New England 300. Jarrett finished third in the race, but his car flunked the height test after the race and he was docked 25 Winston Cup championship points. His crew chief, Todd Parrott, was fined $25,000. (Sam Sharpe)

Right: A NASCAR official holds up a carburetor restrictor plate, which is used at Talladega and Daytona to limit the air-fuel mixture in the engine and cut horsepower nearly in half. It is also one area of the car that teams have tried hard to circumvent over the years. (Tom Copeland)

NASCAR president Mike Helton (left) and managing director of competition Gary Nelson are the two men credited with greatly standardizing the inspection process and narrowing the "gray area" of the NASCAR Winston Cup rulebook over the past decade. (DBP photo)

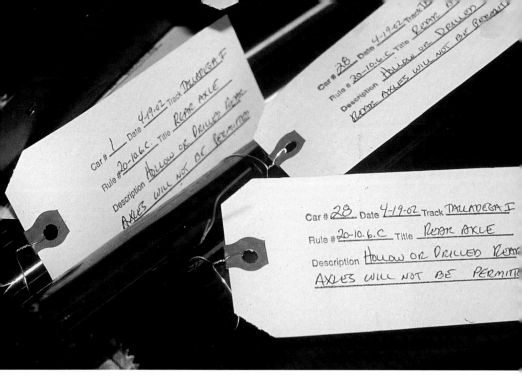

Car # 1 Date 4-19-02 Track Talladega F
Rule # 20-10.6.C. Title REAR AXLE
Description Hollow or Drilled Rear
Axles will not be Permitted

Car # 28 Date 4-19-02 Track Talladega I
Rule # 20-10.6.C Title REAR AXLE
Description Hollow or Drilled Rear
Axles will not be Permitted

Car # 28 Date 4-19-02 Track TALLADEGA I
Rule # 20-10.6.C Title REAR AXLE
Description Hollow or Drilled Rear
Axles will not be Permitted

Above: *A stash of confiscated rear axles and other parts taken from the cars of Ricky Rudd, Steve Park, Kyle Petty and others were put on display for other teams to inspect at Talladega in 2002. (Sam Sharpe)*
Below: *NASCAR's Gary Nelson (right) and John Darby (center) show off an experimental – and illegal – electronic traction control device at Daytona in 2002. The part was not taken from a Winston Cup team, but purchased from an outside vendor trying to sell it to teams. (Tom Copeland)*

I'm not saying who did all this. I was aware of it. I knew about it. Did I work on it? I wasn't exactly sitting back with my feet on the desk."

As bad as rules were bent and even broken in the 1980s, even worse was the feeling in the garage that there was a tremendous inconsistency in NASCAR policing and enforcement, and some teams found out better than others how to play the game and work the rules to their advantage.

"There used to be a lot of big fuel cells," added driver Jimmy Spencer. "I've known guys who had 25 gallons in a [22-gallon] fuel cell. You always wondered why they could run four or five extra laps."

Others pressed their advantage in the area of aerodynamics, where NASCAR had gradually expanded its use of body templates from one in 1967 to about half a dozen by the mid-1980s.

"We learned a lot [about aerodynamics] in the 1980s," said Barry Dodson, who as Rusty Wallace's crew chief led the Missouri driver to his only Winston Cup championship in 1989. Dodson and other smart crew chiefs quickly figured out they could alter their car's body profile in places where NASCAR didn't check and pick up huge aerodynamic advantages, either in the form of less speed-robbing drag at Daytona and Talladega, or much more downforce everywhere else, which dramatically improved handling at slower tracks. Even where NASCAR put templates, teams had up to half an inch of leeway, enough difference to have profound effects on a 180 mph race car.

"We gained a lot of downforce early on," Dodson said, "In the mid-to late-'80s we had some people beat pretty bad. And we knew it. We had them beat aerodynamically, and we took advantage of it. In their [NASCAR's] defense, they didn't have enough templates. They [NASCAR] finally caught on to it."

Another team way ahead of the curve aerodynamically in the mid-1980s was Richard Childress Racing, the team Dale Earnhardt would score six of his seven Winston Cup championships with from 1986 to 1994. Part of the team's success, undeniably, was Earnhardt's superb driving skill and fierce determination to win. But some of it was his team's superiority on the aerodynamic downforce front.

"The No. 3 car [Earnhardt's] was probably one of the ones smart enough to do [aero work]," said former crew chief Larry McReynolds. "There's no telling how narrow they had the C posts, the rear window posts, on their car, which was just dumping air to that rear spoiler." And the more efficiently the air was channeled to the huge rear spoiler, the more firmly it pushed the rear end of the car to the track. And better grip meant faster lap times and, ultimately, more victories.

"Earnhardt was winning a bunch of races and a bunch of championships. Finally, one day somebody [at NASCAR] either noticed it or a few other people did and NASCAR said we better do something about this," McReynolds said. "They came out with a C post template. After they did, the 3 car wasn't winning quite as many races. I'm not saying that's the reason they quit winning as much, but it made a difference."

Conversely, NASCAR sometimes interceded if a car model or make was uncompetitive and helped even out the field. "A good example of that is the 1985–88 Oldsmobile that was racing in the Winston Cup series at that time," said aerodynamicist Louis Duncan, who for many years was Ford's Winston Cup aerodynamicist and from 1998 to 2001 did all the aerodynamic development work for Richard Childress Racing, Dale Earnhardt Inc., and Andy Petree Racing. "The rear deck was short and the quarter panels were very narrow. And the car was not very competitive because the rear end didn't make enough downforce. One of the things that we did—it was not classified as cheating, it was classified as working in the gray areas where NASCAR gives you some leeway—we made the deck six inches longer, and we made the quarter panels wider so that it would look like a wider deck to the air.

"There were no cross templates at that time, and I still remember Dick Beaty putting his wooden template on the car and saying, 'I'll be damned, somebody cut six inches off my template,'" Duncan continued. "What he was saying was, he knew that the performance of the Oldsmobile at that time was not as good and he could see that we had lengthened the rear deck, but he thought that was within bounds. So that's not what I would call cheating, it's what I would call being given some leeway where you need some leeway."

Still, sometimes the tweaking went too far. Ironically, McReynolds said, Earnhardt's team might have gotten nabbed by getting too aggressive. Perhaps, he said, the team tinkered with the roof contours just a little and then, emboldened by their success, gradually got more and more aggressive in their modifications until other teams figured it out and complained to NASCAR or NASCAR inspectors noticed it themselves.

"It ticks me off," said McReynolds of teams who pushed the edge too far. "For instance, if we prove that pulling the corner of the roof on the cars down is good [aerodynamically], you don't want to go so crazy that it's blatant and they [NASCAR] get to looking. I have grabbed many crew chiefs and said, 'Man, don't do that. All you're doing is throwing us all under the bus. I understand you've pulled the roof down four inches and that's great, but you're not going to get that through inspection. All you're going to do is get them on all of us, and we're going to lose everything we've got. Tune it down a little bit. Take that inch and a half that we know is good, but don't try to take that four inches.'"

In other words, "cheat neat," just like Richard Petty advocated in 1965. Of course, when there were no templates to measure what Childress was doing, it wasn't exactly cheating. In fact, the car owner claimed the black No. 3 Chevrolet was scrutinized most closely in inspection when it was most successful. "When we won 10 or 11 races a year, we knew we had to be right," Childress said. "'Cause we knew at the end of the day we were going to get inspected. And that's NASCAR's job. When one team is beating everybody, they have to do a more thorough job and stay on top of everything on that car, because they know that the teams are looking at it as well. It's harder for a guy who is winning to cheat. You know, they say, 'Well, he's got soft tires or he's running this or he's running that.' They're checked by everybody. Even your competitors are looking at you," Childress said.

But if Earnhardt, Childress, and company attracted a lot of scrutiny during their halcyon days in the 1980s, it was even worse for Bill Elliott during his famous 1985 season, when he won 11 races and became the first driver to claim the $1 million "Winston Million" bonus by scoring victories at Daytona, Talladega, and Darlington.

When Elliott came back from two laps down under green-flag conditions to score an improbable victory at Talladega, his car became the target of rumors, speculation, and increasingly zealous post-race inspections for the rest of the season and beyond, a degree of attention that to this day the team says cost it the 1985 Winston Cup championship. The team spent so much time trying to rebuild its cars after post-race inspection that burnout set in, leading to a slump late in the season, especially on short tracks. But on the superspeedways, Elliott's Thunderbird was untouchable.

There were many theories about why Elliott ran so well at superspeedways: Some said engine builder Ernie Elliott coaxed more horsepower out of the team's Ford engines than anyone else; others say it was aerodynamics.

"Everybody thought he was doing something crazy," Humpy Wheeler, the president of Lowe's Motor Speedway, said of Elliott's all-conquering Ford Thunderbird. "In February 1985 at Daytona, somebody came up to me and said, 'Bill Elliott wants to see you in his trailer.' So, I went over there.

"He said, 'I don't know what to do with this car. It is absolutely flying, and I know they [NASCAR] are going to come down on me. And I haven't done anything to this car.'

"I said, 'Well, you've just got to run it like it is and let things work themselves out.' What it was was what we ended up calling ducktailing. That car body was so aerodynamic that, when the air came off the back of it, rather than come straight back it was coming back like this [Wheeler brings his hands together in a V shape]. That's why people couldn't draft him. They'd get up there to draft that car and it would just stop them. That was not an infringement of the rules as much as it was simply a different body style that did a quirky thing, which led to a lot of people cheating that year to try to catch up with him. It caught up with him at Talladega, because he makes two laps up under the green. That did it. That right there ushered in the [new more aerodynamic] back window for the GM cars the following year, but there was a tremendous amount of cheating going on in that period trying to catch Bill Elliott. And, for a while, he didn't know what he was doing."

Or did he?

Aerodynamicist Louis Duncan thinks he did. "Bill Elliott's car was so fast at Talladega that it lapped the field under green twice. He obviously had many good things. He had good pit stops, he had good motors, good bodies, everything about the car was really right," Duncan said. "At that time, there was a long template, a wooden template, no cross templates, and no specific height measurements. That particular car probably maxed out the gray area without being officially cheated up. It was actually a smaller car than the rest of the Thunderbirds. The roof height was lower and the body was narrower. It had been lowered and narrowed so that it was approximately 7/8 scale of a full-size car."

Duncan said, in his mind at least, aero work did not constitute cheating. "Cheating is where you have an illegal shock or you do something that's intentionally against the rules. NASCAR allows gray areas and a little bit of leeway and a little bit of tolerance on the templates," he said. "Working within that tolerance and leeway is not cheating, it's working . . . to make your car as good as you can make it." Arguably, Duncan's interpretation is a liberal and charitable one. Almost any reasonable person would conclude that if, and it's a big if, Elliott's car was indeed substantially smaller than those of the competition, it would constitute a substantial and illegal advantage.

Not that it would be the first time anyone had tried such a trick, of course, Smokey Yunick's 1968 Daytona car was undersized, and in the early 1960s, teams already were trying to drop the noses of their race cars as low as possible at superspeedways.

When asked if it were possible to get away with running an undersized body back then, NASCAR Managing Director of Competition Gary Nelson, who in 1985 was a crew chief competing against Elliott, put it this way: "All I know was I had the same opportunity to put my car through the same inspection process that Elliott's car went through. They were just smarter than me that day." He declined to elaborate.

To this day, Bill Elliott remains vague on the specifics of his 1985 performance. "We were able to bring the sport to the next level and focus on certain things that either other people didn't think of or weren't willing to work for or whatever," he said at Daytona in 2001, a loosely phrased way of saying he outfoxed the competition.

Whatever the source of Elliott's success, his car passed both pre- and post-race inspection at Talladega that day, so by NASCAR's definition it was legal. But the team came under incredible scrutiny for the rest of the 1985 season.

"I think that [Talladega] said a lot to NASCAR about what we could do and the potential that was there," said Bill's brother Dan, who built gears and changed tires for Elliott's team, which was owned by the late Michigan industrialist Harry Melling. "I honestly think that's the reason the car was picked apart after a lot of wins.

"The only blessing I can say that we had was, I guess, some of the inspectors were real fair-minded about the competition. They [NASCAR] did a lot of things that year specifically aimed at us, just to slow us down. The only thing that slowed us down was physical burnout, because there were so few of us."

The team's dominance even earned them a stern rebuke from NASCAR President Bill France Jr. At Darlington in the spring of 1985, the Elliotts were summoned to France's office at the track. "Very little was said," recalled Dan Elliott. "The only thing I can remember him (France) saying was, 'You will not come here and stink up our show.' He said we could win the race, but not by a lap. In other words, we wouldn't embarrass the field."

This was exactly the same kind of heavy-handed treatment that Kiekhaefer endured in the mid-1950s and Jeff Gordon would encounter in 1998: Win a lot and you become a target of the inspectors. "Elliott came in there and won 11 races in

'85," said Bob Moore. "Everyone was sure that Ernie found an illegal way to get a lot of horsepower. Talladega was a perfect example. There is no way they were supposed to be able to do what they did at Talladega. [NASCAR] supposedly destroyed four or five engines trying to find out, so Ernie couldn't put 'em back together. A lot of people are under the impression that they let Elliott get away with it, or in 1998, they let Gordon get away with it, or they let Petty get away with it. That is not the case. NASCAR is doing everything they can."

Ultimately, Elliott and his team set many records in 1985, but came up 11 points short of a Winston Cup title. Whether they lost the title because NASCAR put them under such intense scrutiny or whether they won as often as they did because they had an edge over other teams is open to debate. Likely, it was both.

And if that wasn't enough controversy for one season, there was the inaugural running of "The Winston," a high-dollar no-points race NASCAR bills as its all-star event. The racers who compete in it have their own, more blunt description: They call it "checkers or wreckers." Win or crash trying.

The Winston, which is held at Lowe's Motor Speedway, is the brainchild of sponsor R. J. Reynolds Tobacco Company and its racing director, the late T. Wayne Robertson, and Humpy Wheeler. Like Robertson, who came up through the ranks as a show car driver, Wheeler is an extraordinary promoter, a man with a keen sense of what fans want. He successfully blends elements of P. T. Barnum, Big Bill France, and Vince McMahon at his races.

Although the precise format has varied somewhat over the years, The Winston's formula is a crowd pleaser. Unlike the lengthy races on NASCAR's "official" schedule, The Winston is a collection of three short sprints, ending with a big-buck, winner-take-all 10-lap shootout at the end. Every competitor is either a prior race winner or series champion, meaning the field truly is the best of the best.

And because this is a non-points race, it doesn't count in the Winston Cup standings. Drivers have absolutely no incentive to stroke around the track and pick up a top-five or top-10 finish for a bunch of Winston Cup points. No, you either win The Winston or you lose, nothing in between. The only things up for grabs are bucketloads of cash and bragging rights, two commodities that Winston Cup teams take very seriously. And that means drivers will take big risks on the track, and crew chiefs big ones in the garage.

Not surprisingly, the name of Junior Johnson figured prominently in the inaugural running of The Winston. In 1985, Darrell Waltrip and Jeff Hammond were driver and crew chief, respectively, for Johnson's team, one of 12 competing and a team seemingly headed for defeat, trailing Harry Gant by some three seconds late in the race.

Miraculously, Waltrip ran down Gant late and won the race and $200,000, the biggest prize money of the season. Just as he crossed the finish line, Waltrip's engine exploded, its innards ripped apart, rendering it unsuitable for post-race inspection given the severe damage to its cylinder walls—and the impossibility, therefore, of accurately measuring its displacement.

During post-race interviews, Waltrip attributed his sudden burst of late-race speed to a severe tongue-lashing from Junior over the radio. But based on his stunning and unexpected performance improvement in the last few laps, folks in the garage had suspicions that something more creative might be afoot, mainly a wildly oversized engine that Waltrip nursed through the early stages of the race, "stroking it" in racing vernacular, before hammering it late to secure the win.

It was also widely suspected that Waltrip "clutched" his Chevrolet's engine, a technique racers use to blow up motors. Simply put, if a driver keeps the accelerator wide open with his right foot while simultaneously depressing the clutch pedal with his left foot, he can turn an otherwise perfectly good race engine into a worthless pile of junk. Of course, one could never prove whether or not the engine was oversized, or whether or not Waltrip deliberately blew it up, but the principals involved would laugh about it later.

During a rain delay in the 2001 running of The Winston, Waltrip and Hammond, now commentators for Fox's NASCAR television coverage, had a chuckle over the events of 1985. "We won that first race in '85 with an engine that even today is called into question," Waltrip said, struggling to keep a straight face.

"We got to keep the trophy, we got to keep the check, we must've been legal!" Hammond shot back, laughing. But in a 1998 interview with *Daytona Beach News-Journal* racing reporter Godwin Kelly, Hammond was pretty blunt about the extralegal exploits of his former boss, Junior Johnson. "He was relentless about being creative," Hammond told Kelly. "Everybody said, 'He's cheating, he's cheating.' But that's an unfair statement when you realize that lots of times people like Junior created the rules we're dealing with today."

In Hammond's mind it was self-defense of sorts. "There was not an exact print of this or that being wrong," he explained. In other words, Johnson's belief was that if the rule book did not expressly forbid something, by definition it must be OK to do it. And besides, Hammond said, everybody else was cheating, so he'd do it, too. "Junior figured, why not take it there? Many times when Junior did something, it was to counter what somebody else was doing," Hammond said. "If you get into a war, and somebody starts throwing hand grenades at you, what are going to do, throw rocks back at them? No. You get yourself an airplane and drop a bigger load on the enemy. That's how Junior raced."

"I was all over. I was over that car from one end to the other," Johnson admitted. "If you were checking the front end this week, I'd be checking the back end. Next week I'd be back on the front end. I never quit. I stayed constantly at it. I picked at the car. A lot of the rules today are from things they [NASCAR] caught me with. The things they caught me with were not really cheating; it was innovation. They did not have rules [for] 90 percent of it. I studied the rule book to see where I could go and not have any trouble, and that's what I did."

Usually. Occasionally where he went was a little more innovative than what was allowed by any measure.

"When bigger tracks started coming on and they had better equipment, they started putting in these platform scales," recalled Bud Moore of one episode in the mid-1980s. "You ran the car across the scale, and it weighed half of it at a time. We were at Richmond. Darrell was driving for Junior. We go across the scales. [NASCAR Chief Inspector] Dick Beaty told me, 'I'm going to weigh the cars today. I'm going to catch you cheating so-and-sos.' I got down there and crossed the scales and was 20 pounds light. They made me put 20 pounds in the car. Some came across 30, 40 pounds light.

"But they caught Darrell, he came across 220 pounds light. He was so light he couldn't get enough lead gathered up from everybody to put enough weight in the car. So he missed qualifying. It was funny. I laughed so much. Jeff Hammond, he was running around everywhere that day looking for lead to go in the car. I said, 'Well, you cheating son of a bitch. I can see getting by with 10 or 20 pounds, but 220?'

"He said, 'Well, if you're going to cheat, you might as well cheat.' From that day on, you never got away with being much more than 10 pounds light."

"Well, they filled the frame rail up with buckshot, and they put a spring release on the frame rail. We went to North Wilkesboro, and the minute the race started, Kyle pulled the lever and dumped all this buckshot on the track and made the car about 300 pounds lighter." —Felix Sabates

Chapter 6

*I look at cheating as
something that's done to get
an unfair advantage. What
was done on our car didn't
give us an advantage on
anybody. It wasn't like we had
a big engine or illegal tires.*

—Mark Martin

1990–1995
Cracking Down

O f all the teams in NASCAR's history, none has paid a higher price for rules violations than Roush Racing, violations that many would argue deserved far less severe penalties than the team received.

Since entering NASCAR in 1988 after successful stints in a host of motorsports, team founder and owner Jack Roush fully expected to add to the 24 championships he had won in Sports Car Club of America and International Motor Sports Association competition. Instead, he twice had NASCAR titles snatched from his grasp because of alleged rules violations. The first was for an infraction that didn't materially affect his car's performance, and the second was something Roush swears to this day was never illegal to begin with.

The first incident occurred on a bone-chillingly cold weekend in Richmond, Virginia, at the Pontiac Excitement 400 in February 1990. Roush's driver, Mark Martin, claimed victory in that event, thanks in large part to a savvy strategic decision by then–crew chief Robin Pemberton, who called for Martin to make a two-tire pit stop during the final caution period of the race. While most of the other front-runners took four tires, Martin took the lead under yellow and went on to win, besting archrival Dale Earnhardt in the process.

But four-and-a-half hours after the race, NASCAR ruled that Martin's carburetor spacer—a piece that fits between the carburetor and the intake manifold and positions the carburetor at the correct height—was 2.5 inches high, half an inch taller than the legal maximum.

At most, the extra half-inch was worth two to three horsepower, hardly the difference between winning and losing. And the car already had passed muster twice, receiving approval from NASCAR officials after the customary qualifying and pre-race inspections.

Worse yet, the infraction was avoidable. Because of an apparent mix-up in communications between Pemberton and the crew, the 2.5-inch spacer was bolted to the manifold. Had the team welded an extra half an inch onto the manifold and then bolted a 2-inch spacer on top of it, the car would have been totally legal with the carburetor sitting at exactly the same height.

Of all the brazen cheating in NASCAR's history—everything from big engines and soaked tires to undersized, wind-cheating bodies—this was about as close to an innocent mistake as a team could make, one that no one argued affected the outcome of the race. Yet it cost the driver, the team, and its crew chief dearly.

Martin was stripped of 46 Winston Cup points, the difference between his first-place finish and the 10th-place car, which was the last to finish on the lead lap. Roush Racing was fined $40,000—the largest fine in the sport's history up to that point—and crew chief Robin Pemberton was suspended for 30 days by team owner Jack Roush, a suspension that was lifted after just 48 hours.

"It took my breath [when Roush issued the suspension]," Pemberton told *NASCAR Winston Cup Scene* managing editor Deb Williams, "It caught me off guard. You can be on top of things one minute, and it can be over with the next. This particular situation could turn into losses of millions of dollars in sponsorships [and] prize money."

Little did he know just how prescient he would prove to be.

Martin would eventually lose the 1990 Winston Cup championship to Dale Earnhardt by just 26 points, surrendering the points lead in the season's penultimate race at Phoenix. And while Earnhardt would go on to claim a record-tying seven championships, Martin is still looking for his first. That season, and again in 1997, Martin would go to the final race of the year in Atlanta with a chance at the title, only to come up short.

"People are going to say we are cheating to win, but it's not like that," Martin said after the Richmond ruling. "I look at cheating as something that's done to get an unfair advantage. What was done on our car didn't give us an advantage on anybody. It wasn't like we had a big engine or illegal tires."

A decade later, Pemberton would admit, "I still have nightmares about Richmond."

Roush appealed the suspension to the National Stock Car Racing Commission, a NASCAR-appointed oversight committee, which heard the case March 14. Such appeals rarely are successful; the commission is regarded by many within the sport, correctly so, as little more than a rubber stamp for the France family. Not surprisingly, John Cooper, Dan Greenwood, and Bob Smith, the three commission members who heard the case, ruled against Roush the next day, saying the bolted-on carburetor spacer was in clear violation of the rules, even if it offered little, if any, measurable performance gain. Officially, a team was caught breaking the rules, and after the appropriate investigation, punishment was levied.

Of course, like any controversy in NASCAR, this one led to plenty of rumors and speculation. "The stiff penalty instituted by NASCAR led most people in the garage area to believe there was more wrong with the car than simply an illegal carburetor spacer. "The most often heard rumor was the team had left-side tires on the right side," wrote *Scene*'s Williams, which would have given the car a handling advantage. She added that there was also speculation that the engine was too big. Neither offense was ever proven.

In fact, a week later at Rockingham, NASCAR Winston Cup Director Dick Beaty tried to dispel the gossip. "For everyone's information and to stop the rumors that are going around, the Roush team had a legal engine," Beaty told a group of reporters. "It was a 357.189 cubic-inch engine, which is well under the maximum 358 cubic inches that's allowable. You may rest assured no big engine will get by Dick Beaty. Also, to end another rumor, the team didn't have left-side tires on the right side of the car."

Still, the punishment hardly seemed to fit the crime. "I hate to say it, but the carburetor was the only thing [illegal]. I swear to God," Pemberton said. "I would think there had to be something else [because of the fine] but there wasn't."

Maybe, maybe not. In an interview with an engine builder who spoke on the condition of anonymity, *Scene* editor Gary McCredie suggested NASCAR politics might have played a key role in the severity of the penalty. "I think maybe [Martin's] car failed too many times going through inspection at Daytona Beach [two weeks before Richmond]," McCredie quoted the engine builder as saying. "It kept coming back fudged up. There were a lot of things [wrong with it]. You ask them how many times the car failed pre-race inspection. I think it had to go through six times. There's sort of an honor system there, and I think they [the NASCAR inspectors] kind of got tired of being abused. Perhaps there had been some restrictor plate or carburetor hanky-panky at Daytona that had been dismissed with a stern warning that went ignored."

Another theory was that Roush's team was caught because a rival crew chief spotted the too-tall carburetor spacer and had his team owner personally contact NASCAR President Bill France Jr., who in turn alerted inspectors about the transgression. Whatever the reasons or motivations, Roush and Martin paid dearly. There are some who believe that neither Martin nor Roush ever fully recovered from the Richmond incident, and that's why they never claimed a Winston Cup championship.

If the 1990s began with Roush Racing, a relatively new Winston Cup team, in trouble with NASCAR, a well-known repeat offender would fight the law again, and this time, the law would win.

The first running of The Winston in 1985 may have represented Junior Johnson's best moment of skirting NASCAR's rules, but the 1991 edition of NASCAR's all-star event clearly was the low point. By now, Johnson had a different driver, Geoff Bodine; a different crew chief in Tim Brewer; and he was racing Fords again instead of the Chevrolets that he ran in Waltrip's heyday or the Oldsmobiles he campaigned with Cale Yarborough from 1976 to 1978, when he became the only car owner in Winston Cup history to win three consecutive championships.

When Bodine was injured in a crash during practice prior to The Winston, Johnson tapped journeyman Tommy Ellis to fill in for him. Ellis did OK in the race, but came home a mediocre 13th among 20 cars competing at The Winston. But in post-race inspection, NASCAR discovered Johnson was running an oversized engine in Ellis's car, one that measured 361 cubic inches instead of the permitted 358.

"At Charlotte they caught us with an engine that was three cubic inches bigger than it was supposed to be," Johnson said. "But that was a mechanic's error. It was not an intentional thing. It was just a mistake that the guy did on the engine. He picked up the wrong crankshaft and put it in the engine. It was a mistake on his side, but NASCAR caught it."

According to Johnson, engine builders use different combinations of bore and stroke when building engines. These different combinations produce different characteristics of throttle response, torque, and horsepower, and some combinations are better suited for specific tracks than others. At the half-mile Martinsville Speedway, for example, where drivers are on and off the throttle constantly, a team would run a much different engine than they would use at Daytona or Talladega, where the cars run at full throttle virtually all race long.

Johnson's contention was that his engine man mistakenly put together an engine that was longer stroke and big bore, resulting in a minor discrepancy in displacement. The argument is certainly plausible, even given Johnson's long and colorful record of prior infractions.

But NASCAR had to levy a punishment against Johnson, since his team had violated what was one of the sport's sacrosanct rules: Don't run big engines. Although this rule had been liberally violated in earlier decades, following the Richard Petty incident at Charlotte eight years earlier, NASCAR knew it had to crack down on flagrant cheaters, so it mandated 12-week suspensions for teams caught running oversized engines. Unless, of course, politics interfered, as was the case here.

Johnson's car was sponsored by Budweiser, the official beer of NASCAR and a subsidiary of Anheuser-Busch, whose Busch beer brand was the title sponsor of NASCAR's AAA division, the Busch Series. Budweiser also was title sponsor of three Winston Cup races that season, including one scheduled for two weeks after The Winston in Dover, Delaware. The prevailing sentiment in the garage was that NASCAR would not humiliate one of its biggest corporate benefactors by banning its team car for 12 races.

NASCAR bent its own rules rather drastically. Ellis was a fill-in, not a permanent member of the team, so his suspension was lifted, while Johnson and Brewer were slapped on the hands with four race bans. In a move truly worthy of comparison to something that would go on in the World Wrestling Federation, Johnson transferred ownership of his team to his then-wife Flossie, changed the car's number from 11 to 97 and ran the next four races, two with Ellis behind the wheel and then two more, both top-10 finishes, with the recently healed Bodine.

Roush and Johnson weren't the only creative minds in the garage that NASCAR was fighting with at that point. Gary Nelson, who had raised eyebrows with some of his innovations while at DiGard Racing in the late 1970s and early 1980s, was a constant thorn in Beaty's side.

Nelson remained at DiGard until late in 1985, when he joined Hendrick Motorsports. The following February, he prepared Geoff Bodine's Daytona 500–winning Chevrolet for Hendrick. But after three up-and-down seasons at Hendrick, Nelson was ready for a change and found himself joining forces with Team Sabco car owner Felix Sabates and driver Kyle Petty in 1989. It wasn't long before some of Nelson's old tricks surfaced again.

"I was very naive in the early days," said Sabates, a colorful and often controversial Cuban expatriate and one of the few true eccentric personalities left in the sport. "I went to lunch with my crew chief—that was in the early, early days, so you can figure out who the crew chief was—and one of my mechanics, and he said, 'We've got to stop at an ammunition store.'

"I said, 'An ammunition store?'

"And he said, 'Yeah.' I figured they wanted to buy some shotgun shells or something. I pulled in there, and they came out with three or four bags of really heavy stuff. I said, 'What's that?'

"'Buckshot.'

"'Really? What's that for?'

"'You don't need to know.'

"Well, they filled the frame rail up with buckshot, and they put a spring release on the frame rail. We went to North Wilkesboro, and the minute the race started, Kyle pulled the lever and dumped all this buckshot on the track and made the car about 300 pounds lighter. After the race I remember trying to get across the track and people were slipping on the buckshot, but they don't know who did it," Sabates said.

According to Sabates, the old buckshot trick was one of just many tools in Nelson's arsenal.

"Gary spent probably 50 percent of his time trying to figure out how to circumvent the system and 50 percent of the time doing it the right way," said Sabates. "Gary was great. I still say, to this day, that Gary was the best at calling a race. There's no one who could even come close. Gary was a genius with the bodies. He wasn't too good with the engines, because that wasn't his forte. Gary did a lot of creative things with our bodies. We showed up one time at Talladega with a car that was one-third Pontiac, one-third Oldsmobile and one-third Chevy.... We went to Talladega and kicked everybody's butt until we got involved in a wreck and Kyle broke his leg."

But by 1991, Nelson decided he'd been a crew chief long enough. The intensity of the job got to him, as it does to most in the sport eventually. "What you have to understand to be a good racer, whether it's a crew chief, a race driver, or an engine builder, to be in this garage at all, you have to be good," said Nelson. "But to be the best in this garage, you have to race 24 hours a day. Every second of your life is consumed with making your car win. If you're the engine builder, the driver, the crew chief, whatever, your life becomes winning that next race."

At this point, Dick Beaty was ready for a change, too. So as Beaty was preparing for retirement, Sabates was helping Nelson land the job as Winston Cup director.

"I'm the one who called Bill France way back then and said, 'Bill, we're going to part company, and I think if you guys need a guy for the job, Gary Nelson's the man,'" the Team Sabco car owner said. "I suffered because of my recommendation, but I'm the one who recommended NASCAR hire Gary."

The move was heartily endorsed by Beaty. "Fellas, I know Gary will do a good job because he knows all the tricks," Beaty said in introducing Nelson as his replacement. The two spent a year working together in 1992, with Nelson serving as an understudy before assuming the helm for the start of the 1993 season. He was the ideal man for the job, as Beaty had pointed out and others agreed.

"The first thing they did was they went out and got the biggest cheater they could find," said former driver Buddy Baker. "Gary Nelson was a very, very sharp person."

More importantly, "He knows how to catch these guys, and if they do enough, he'll get 'em," Baker said. At the 1993 Daytona 500, Nelson did just that, when virtually every car entered failed inspection. Competitors soon got the message that there was a new sheriff in town.

It wasn't long, though, before Nelson saw how complex life was on the other side of the badge. For one thing, eliminating the ambivalence in NASCAR's rule book was nowhere near as easy as he thought it would be.

"I was naive enough to assume I could eliminate the gray area in the rule book," he said. "I'd just rewrite all the rules so there was no way anyone could interpret them in a different way than I had intended. That didn't happen. . . . [Now] I try my best to eliminate gray areas and say, 'OK, here's the line, don't cross it.' You do that with words when you write a rule. Well, you have a picture in your mind when you write it of what you want to see, and you try to take your picture from your mind to the page.

"Somebody else picks up that book out of the blue, they're supposed to develop the same picture in their mind that I had in my mind when I wrote it. Very seldom does that work that way. The competitor, who is looking at a way to do better on the racetrack, will read it differently and try to find ways to get a little more out of that paragraph or that rule. And so then it becomes a matter of interpretation. Even the rules that I thought were ironclad, no loopholes, no questions, no doubt, still competitors will find a way to say, 'Hey, I read this, and this is what I think it says.'

"So I really understand now that you'll never eliminate the gray areas. You try and try and try, and you find more and more refined ways to get into the gray area. We understand that and we accept that and we do our best to fight it on a weekly basis, but my point probably is best illustrated with the Supreme Court of the United States. They've been in business since the beginning of the Constitution, and they're still trying to interpret it every day," Nelson said.

Of course, even when the rules are clear, some men aren't afraid to challenge those rules. Such was the case in 1994, when NASCAR and Nelson had yet another run-in with Junior Johnson. At the time, Johnson's driver was an energetic, inexperienced, and occasionally reckless youngster named Jimmy Spencer, who was nicknamed "Mr. Excitement" for his wild, aggressive driving. But Spencer enjoyed little success with Johnson's team, and his sponsor, McDonald's, was rumored to be leaving the sport. NASCAR desperately wanted to avoid McDonald's departure. To lose a big name like McDonald's would be bad for business, and many believed NASCAR would do almost anything to keep the fast-food giant in the sport.

Out of nowhere, Spencer suddenly won back-to-back races at Daytona and Talladega in mid-1994, two restrictor-plate races where a resourceful man like Johnson could work his magic. Though never proven, the prevalent rumor at the time was that Johnson's Ford carried an illegal intake manifold, much like the one Hoss Ellington had come up with a decade earlier, which allowed the car to make extra horsepower.

The theory was that NASCAR knew the car was illegal but looked the other way, hoping a couple of victories would convince McDonald's to stay in the sport. In the end, McDonald's stayed as both a car sponsor and, more importantly, an "official status" sponsor, which means the hamburger chain paid

NASCAR a seven-figure annual sum to be able to call itself "the official fast-food of NASCAR."

The conspiracy theorists argued that their point was proven the following February at Daytona. The manifold that was on Spencer's car in 1994 when it won the only two races of his career was declared illegal at the 1995 Daytona 500, when car owner Johnson was fined $45,000 and his crew chief Mike Beam was hit with a $10,000 penalty for not having the inset portion of the intake manifold welded on. Incensed by what he perceived as the ever-increasing influence of politics and corporate interests in the sport, as well as the ever-closer scrutiny cars were receiving in inspection, Johnson would sell his team at the end of 1995 and retire to his farm in Wilkes County, North Carolina.

Other racers were equally incensed that the team was able to get through inspection in 1994 with the same manifold that was declared illegal in 1995.

"They [NASCAR] let him win two races for McDonald's," said John Bickford, the stepfather of four-time Winston Cup Champion Jeff Gordon and the man who managed Gordon's career until mid-1995. "There was a perception that NASCAR overlooked the Junior Johnson team and allowed McDonald's to win two races so they stayed in the sport and they maintained an official status. Jimmy Spencer won his two races, and if you go back and look at the videotape, he just hammered them. It wasn't like it was his slick ability to handle the air, as Dale Earnhardt was known for or Bill Elliott or now Jeff Gordon, who are some of the best drafters and users of air in the industry. But it was Jimmy Spencer, Mr. Excitement's style to motor by everybody. Yeah, right. He had an extra 30 horsepower on everybody. He had a slider manifold."

A slider manifold is something of a catch-all nickname that refers to several types of illegal, movable devices designed to boost horsepower by improving airflow, usually in a restrictor-plate motor. These include restrictor plates with machined center sections that slide back and forth via a driver-controlled cable to allow extra air into the motor, carburetor spacers that are machined to slide back and forth in their entirety on the mounting studs (again, these are driver controlled), and movable internal plenums hidden deep inside the base of the intake manifold.

NASCAR has always maintained that Johnson's car was legal when it won the two races and that it made absolutely no concessions or did anything wrong to encourage McDonald's to remain in the sport.

Johnson and Spencer are a little more forthcoming. "I probably only got caught legally one time. That was at Daytona in 1995," Johnson said. "We got caught with a manifold that we knew NASCAR had let scoot through on another car [Spencer's, the year before]. We got caught at Daytona with it. I told the crew to put the regular manifold on the car regardless of how it ran, and they got behind and didn't take it off and went through inspection and they [NASCAR] caught them."

"When I came to drive for Junior, he said, 'You're going to win on the speedways because I'm going to build you a car,'" Spencer said. "We had an opportunity to win all four super-speedway races that year, and it was because of the car

Junior built. He knew how to make these cars go fast and how to get the edge and things like that. Junior was one of the best at it there ever was. He was hard work. Junior would try to figure out ways of winning races. To say that he won a lot of races cheating, no. He'd work hard trying to make the most horsepower he could make. He'd work hard trying to make a car body the best it could be, at Daytona or wherever we went.

"Junior was one of the best at it there ever was," said Spencer. "The thing about him was he quit this sport because of the rules. Junior, it wasn't never cheating to him, it was just reading the rules a little different. I think our sport has lost a lot of ingenuity that has gone into it."

While Johnson was preparing to sell his team, the sport's next emerging superstar team had its first serious run-in with NASCAR. In the 1995 Coca-Cola 600 at Charlotte Motor Speedway, Jeff Gordon's Hendrick Motorsports Chevrolet lost its right-front hub on lap 80, causing Gordon to end the race in 33rd place. A subsequent inspection by NASCAR found that the hub in question was a lightweight piece that had not been approved by NASCAR. Crew chief Ray Evernham admitted his decision to run the piece was a poor one.

Asked if he'd appeal the record $60,000 fine handed down by NASCAR, Evernham was quoted by *NASCAR Winston Cup Scene* associate editor Tom Stinson as saying, "What's to appeal? It's black and white. It was on the car. What's to appeal? It was a safety issue. Thank God nobody got hurt. I don't see where there's room to appeal. It was a serious violation. It was a cut-and-dried issue. When I think of what could have happened, it's a sickening feeling. That's something I just have to live with and go on."

Evernham went on to say the team hadn't used the offending piece in earlier races, and it was his decision alone to try it at Charlotte. "This should not be a reflection on Jeff, Rick Hendrick, or this team," Evernham told Stinson. "It was my responsibility. I'm this week's ass." Like most illegal parts controversies, this one was eerily reminiscent of one that happened years earlier, specifically when Maurice Petty took the rap for brother Richard's big engine at the same track 12 years earlier.

Still, if Evernham was indeed "this week's ass," he had plenty of company that season. Even more flagrant was the movable rear sheet metal on the Pontiac owned by Bill Davis and driven by Randy LaJoie. The car had a secret hydraulic pump rigged with a line to the clutch pedal. When the driver stepped on the clutch, it engaged a switch that lowered the entire rear deck lid by about half an inch, causing greatly reduced aerodynamic drag. When caught with the illegal device by NASCAR inspectors, crew chief Chris Hussey had a simple explanation: "They were doing their job and we were trying to do ours," he said.

Little more than two months later, Ricky Rudd was caught with a similar device on his car at Talladega, and his team was fined a total of $50,000. "One of our inspectors was under the car and saw some excess grease in a place he thought was unusual," NASCAR spokesman Kevin Triplett told *NASCAR Winston Cup Scene*. "We noticed something wasn't right, and after further inspection, we discovered how the apparatus worked. There was a T-split off the wire from the clutch, part of which would allow the clutch to do its job, while the other half would deliver hydraulic fluid to the cross member of the frame above the rear springs. The line ran through the cross member and frame of the car and to the clutch. There was a set screw apparatus that would allow the car to come through inspection at the proper height. By the time the car comes up to speed and goes into the turns, g-forces and gravity would push the screw down and lower the rear end. Then when the clutch was pumped, it would push hydraulic fluid through and bring the car back to its proper height."

All in all, it was a busy year for inspectors. Gordon would go on to win the 1995 Winston Cup Championship, his first of three in a four-year period. Still, his team would have its share of run-ins with NASCAR in years to come.

Jeff Gordon won the 1997 Winston in a specially designed car with a radical and highly controversial chassis that was declared legal by NASCAR when it raced but outlawed the following week. (DBP photo)

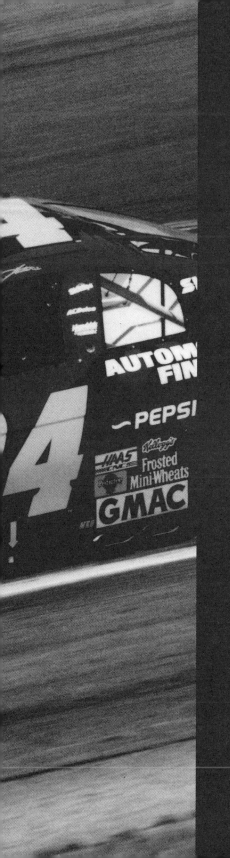

Chapter 7

*It sounds to me like Jack
[Roush] is losing his mind.*

—**Ray Evernham**

1996–1999
Going Public

In the second half of the 1990s, NASCAR again had its hands full trying to sort out exactly who was cheating and who wasn't. Some of the most pitched battles, both on the track and in the inspection lines, involved bitter rivals Jack Roush and Ray Evernham, though they had plenty of company in the scofflaw department.

Roush and NASCAR got into it at Talladega on May 9, 1997, two days prior to the rain-delayed Winston 500. When the Roush Racing Ford driven by Jeff Burton rolled through inspection on that day, NASCAR officials were surprised to find its roof was unlike any they had ever seen on a super-speedway car before.

At the time, NASCAR used four templates to measure roof dimensions: the so-called "long template" that runs the length of the car from nose to rear spoiler and three others that fit across the width of the roof at its front, center, and rear, respectively. The body on Burton's car, a body that was built not by Roush but by an undisclosed third-party vendor, fit all four of NASCAR's templates. Everything else about it, however, was wrong.

The roof flaps, thin strips of sheet metal designed to raise up in the air and keep the car from flipping in the event of a spin, were mounted five inches forward of the NASCAR-mandated location. NASCAR officials admitted this modification offered no performance advantage—after all, they only deployed if the car was out of control—but were incensed nonetheless.

Tampering with a safety feature of the car was one offense they took very, very seriously. Ironically, Roush himself had designed the flaps, working in concert with NASCAR to improve safety in accident conditions.

But in a display that shocked the garage, NASCAR officials literally cut the roof off the car in the garage at Talladega, destroying the car.

Officially the explanation for the stiff punishment, which included a $20,000 fine in addition to the destruction of a $150,000 race car, was that the flaps were improperly mounted. "The fact is, we know the roof flaps work in the position they're supposed to be in," said NASCAR's Kevin Triplett, who had been promoted from his PR capacity to become director of operations, in an interview with *Winston Cup Scene*'s Tom Stinson. "There's no way of knowing whether they would work or not [on Burton's car], and that's a chance we're not willing to take."

Of course, as always in stock-car racing, the reality was a bit more complicated than the public explanation. Several Winston Cup crew chiefs said the roof did indeed fit the four templates, but had been "scalloped"—lowered everywhere except where the templates fit in an attempt to greatly reduce aerodynamic drag.

In fairness to Roush, his team bought the body from an outside supplier, one the team would not do business with again after Talladega. Still, scalloping was not a "gray area" miscalculation. It was an aggressive attempt at chicanery, and NASCAR responded forcefully.

Gary DeHart, crew chief for 1995 Winston Cup champion Terry Labonte, would later call it "the squirreliest thing he'd ever seen in racing." Fellow crew chief Robbie Loomis agreed, saying it was the most outlandish modification he'd ever seen a team try to get through the inspection line.

Burton's car would not be the last outlandish car NASCAR would encounter that year.

At Daytona in July, during practice for the Pepsi 400, NASCAR found movable carburetor mounting studs on John Andretti's Ford, an offense that earned crew chief Tony Furr a stiff $50,000 fine from the sanctioning body.

According to NASCAR, the top half of the studs slid as much as 1/8 inch, which allowed the carburetor to move slightly, improving airflow and giving the engine an extra five horsepower or more. In an interview with *NASCAR Winston Cup Scene*, Andretti's engine builder Tony Santanicola called the penalty "ridiculous," adding, "There's no rule against it. They [NASCAR] just didn't like it."

NASCAR officials disagreed, citing a codicil in the rule book that stated carburetor mounting studs must remain in a specified location.

Furr and Santanicola removed the offending carburetor studs, and Andretti went on to win the race, the first of his NASCAR career, and the first as a car owner for NASCAR legend Cale Yarborough. Unfortunately for the team, NASCAR's fine was upheld on appeal to the National Stock Car Racing Commission.

A year later, at the very same race, it was Team Sabco's turn for trouble. When Sterling Marlin's car went through inspection, NASCAR officials found an intricately machined clear plastic insert at the bottom of the intake manifold, a device designed to improve the flow of the air-fuel mixture from the carburetor into the cylinder heads.

The benefit of the device depended on who you talked to: One crew chief who spoke under the condition of anonymity, said the insert would give the engine an additional 15 to 20 horsepower, or maybe more.

NASCAR officials and other crew chiefs who spoke off the record said the main advantage of the insert was not horsepower, but throttle response: Having the device meant Marlin's engine would come up to full power sooner if he had to back off the throttle and then get back on it quickly in traffic, a frequent problem in the long drafting packs at Daytona and Talladega.

The punishment, predictably, was stiff: Crew chief Scott Eggleston was fined $50,000 and placed on probation until October 20. The scuttlebutt in the garage at the time was the insert took six months and cost $20,000 to develop—and that NASCAR was furious because it was made of clear plastic in an attempt to avoid detection. "It was probably the most blatant thing we've seen in three or four years," NASCAR's Triplett said. "It was pretty far across the line."

And as if anyone needed confirmation of NASCAR's seriousness on the subject, one week after the Daytona race, when the Winston Cup circuit traveled to New Hampshire, seven teams were caught with fuel cell violations. During inspections both before morning practice and afternoon qualifying at Loudon, officials confiscated fuel cells made of too-thin metal from the cars driven by Rich Bickle, Derrike Cope, Rick Mast, Dale Earnhardt, Dale Earnhardt Jr., and Hut Stricklin. Brett Bodine had his fuel cell taken because part of the foam inner liner required for safety reasons had been removed, allowing the car to carry an extra gallon or so of gas—which could be the difference between winning or losing a race.

Those escapades, however, were mere footnotes compared to the ruckus raised by Evernham at the running of the 1997 Winston, when the crew chief engineered the most brilliant act of deception in the history of The Winston, and it was all perfectly legal. In the process, he made fools of the competition and the media with a purpose-built race car that succeeded perfectly in its mission: win the only race in which it would ever appear.

At the time of the 1997 Winston, Evernham was in his fifth full season as crew chief for young phenom Jeff Gordon at the powerhouse Hendrick Motorsports team, and they were on the verge of creating a team every bit as powerful as Richard Petty or Dale Earnhardt had enjoyed in their primes.

For the 1997 Winston, Evernham and his Hendrick Motorsports associates cooked up something special. Gordon's

Chevrolet Monte Carlo carried a special paint scheme promoting Universal Pictures's upcoming movie release, *Jurassic
Park: The Lost World*. The team nicknamed the car T-Rex,
which fans and media alike assumed referred to the dinosaurs
from the movie promoted on the hood of the car. In reality,
the T-Rex was named in honor of Hendrick's lead chassis engineer, Rex Stump, who had designed the chassis. It was so
revolutionary that Evernham invited Winston Cup Director
Gary Nelson to his shop to see ahead of time, to ensure that
the car would be allowed to compete in The Winston. The T-
Rex, you see, was unlike anything NASCAR or Evernham's
fellow competitors had ever seen before.

Basically, the chassis of most stock cars are set up for their
handling to improve over the course of a tire run. At the 1.5-
mile Lowe's Motor Speedway where The Winston is run, for
example, the track also hosts two regular points races annu-
ally, one 600 miles in length, the other 500 miles. Assuming
no caution periods, a stock car typically can go 50 to 60 green-
flag laps at Lowe's before it needs to be pitted for fuel and fresh
tires. Over the length of that run, the car should be set up so
that it gets more to the driver's liking the longer the run lasts,
so the car becomes easier to handle the longer it's driven.

But The Winston is different. At that time the longest seg-
ments were 30 laps each and essentially meaningless to the
night's outcome, because typically the order of the field was
reset at the start of the next segment. In The Winston, the only
part of the race that mattered is the 10-lap sprint at the very
end. For those conditions, what you want is a car that has opti-
mum handling at the start of the run. It needs early speed, not

the long-distance balance a driver would want over a 50-lap run in a conventional race.

The optimal setup is one that gets as much heat into the front tires as quickly as possible, for maximum traction. Over a 50-lap distance, that could cause overheating and blistering, but it's what a car needs to go fast quickly.

So Evernham and Rex designed a radically different suspension system for the T-Rex, with the front shock absorbers mounted as far outboard as possible to get heat in the front tires immediately.

"The car had a lot of different construction features: the way the floor pan and the frame rails were in it," said Evernham. "The car had an aerodynamic advantage and a mechanical suspension advantage. Rex is a pretty smart guy. He just took everything to the maximum, and it ended up being a pretty nice race car. A lot of the suspension components and things like that that are illegal now were all built within the rules then. We had trailing arms with springs in them, all kinds of stuff, but there were no rules about that at that time."

The only race such a setup could succeed in was The Winston. The strategy was genius on two fronts: First off, it worked—Gordon's car won the 10-lap sprint at the end. Second, it was a brilliant diversionary move. Other crew chiefs who saw the car were outraged and stormed into the NASCAR trailer demanding the T-Rex be banned. If not, they'd have to figure out how to replicate the same design in their own cars. The media bought into all the talk that Evernham was cheating and that there were all kinds of trick parts on the car.

And Evernham, who had built a car for one race and one race only, got to publicly wring his hands that NASCAR was setting back his R&D program when it announced after The Winston that it had changed the rules to prevent the T-Rex from ever running again. The reason, Nelson would say later, was simple: "We look at three things. First, does it give an unfair performance advantage? No, it doesn't, because the car wouldn't race anywhere else. Second, is it unsafe? No, there was nothing inherently unsafe about it. Third, does it cost too much? And there's where we had to draw the line, because if every other competitor had to go out and build a car like this, it would drive the price of racing up too high."

Of course, at the time nobody other than Hendrick Motorsports officials and NASCAR officials fully understood that the T-Rex was never intended to be used anywhere other than The Winston. Evernham played up NASCAR's banning of the T-Rex to maximum advantage with the racing media.

"With the new rules [banning the design] the car was just no good," Evernham told David Poole of the *Charlotte Observer*, claiming the T-Rex was a prototype for the team's 1998 chassis. "It has put us a year behind with our chassis program. While we were sent back to the drawing board it has forced us to run a lot of older cars during the first part of the '98 season."

In an article provocatively titled "Where's the line between champion and cheater?" *Orlando Sentinel* reporter Juliet Macur tackled the T-Rex myth. "Its sleek, inventive chassis design made its underbelly more aerodynamic—thus much faster in certain races," She also quoted Evernham as saying he was disappointed the car was banned: "The selfish side of me, the racer side said, 'But hey, why not?' But when the business side of me started thinking about it, I started to agree with them [NASCAR] because it wouldn't have been good for the sport. We would have had a big advantage and won a lot of races."

For John Bickford, 1997's running of The Winston was déjà vu all over again. "When I was a kid and just getting started, 16 or 17, I was getting my ass whipped every week by a guy named Gene Dudley," Bickford said. "At the time, I was thinking he was the biggest cheater out there. When he retired, I bought his stuff. And you know what? It was just normal stuff. But there was no extra [equipment or illegal parts]. He was so focused on everything that made his car work. He was a good driver, his motor was efficient, everything about his whole team was efficient, nothing wasted. Yet we were focused on his cheating, not racing. So therefore he had us buffaloed going in, because our attention was somewhere else. He put a shock on the right-rear of his car and put a spring around it. We figured, OK, he's got himself some special suspension deal. We were designing and getting springs, putting them over our shocks. When I bought his car, I found out it didn't do a damn thing except distract all of us.

"Ray has been in the position where all eyes are on Ray Evernham to see what he's doing, because racers are all copycats. As soon as they see Ray do something, they all go out and do it. They don't know why, but they know if Ray's doing it they got to do it. They're not sure what it does, but they'll figure it [out] down the road. So where is their focus and attention? Ray's focused on going faster on the racetrack, and they're all focused on what Ray's doing. They're automatically behind him."

Having won The Winston and then bamboozled the motorsports media about his intentions afterwards, Evernham recovered from being put "a year behind with our chassis program." His driver, Gordon, went on to claim Winston Cup championships that season and again in 1998, when he won a record-tying 13 races.

But with those 13 victories in 1998 would come a fierce challenge to Evernham's integrity and honesty from Roush, which initiated one of the most contentious and bilious cheating debates in NASCAR's history, a fight that came to be known as "Tiregate."

Tiregate pitted Roush and Evernham, two of the sport's most brilliant and driven personalities, against each other in a high-stakes war of words and wits that polarized fans and competitors and threatened to tear the sport apart as two top teams fought for a championship.

Roush's driver, Mark Martin, had come tantalizing close to two Winston Cup championships, coming up short in the final race of the season at Atlanta twice, in 1990 and 1997. The second time he lost to Jeff Gordon, the driver of the Evernham-prepared Hendrick Motorsports Chevrolets.

The lack of a championship grated on Roush, a proud, talented man who had accumulated a substantial fortune doing research and development for virtually every automaker in the world at his massive Roush Industries facility in Livonia, Michigan.

By 1998, Gordon, Evernham, and the rest of the so-called "Rainbow Warriors" on the Hendrick Motorsports team had become the sport's newest dynasty, winning championships in 1995 and 1997, while finishing a close second in 1996.

Clearly, the teams were intense rivals. Roush had tried to hire Gordon in 1992, but had twice been rebuffed by Bickford, who insisted that any team owner signing Gordon would have to take Evernham with him as crew chief.

"My drivers don't get to pick their crew chiefs. I do that," Roush had told Bickford. Bickford hung up on him.

The genesis of Tiregate came with Evernham's seemingly uncanny ability to make the right decisions about tires in late-race pit stops, probably a crew chief's most important strategic task.

When the race is on the line and drivers come in for what they expect will be their final pit stops, each driver and crew chief must decide whether to take four tires, two tires, or no tires and whether to make any chassis adjustment.

Numerous factors shape these decisions: how many laps are on the current tires, how many laps are left, what the weather is like, how hard the track is to pass on, and a whole host of other variables.

At some tracks, the decision is easy. At Darlington and Rockingham, for example, the track surfaces are so abrasive and hard on tires that teams virtually always change four tires on every pit stop, even if the last set of tires only has 10 laps on them.

Some drivers and crew chiefs are very good at such decisions, but Gordon and Evernham took it to a whole new level in 1998. That May at the Coca-Cola 600 in Charlotte, Gordon took four tires in a late-race pit stop, while Rusty Wallace and the rest of the leaders took two. Gordon, who had not been much of a factor in the race, suddenly came from the tail end of the lead lap, passing nine cars in the final 15 laps to stun the field and secure the victory.

When the Winston Cup circuit moved to Michigan Speedway for the August 16 Pepsi 400, Gordon was on a hot streak, having won the previous three races—with Martin finishing second each time—and seven for the season. He also led the points race and was on track for his third Winston Cup title in four years.

It was an emotionally charged weekend. Martin had lost his father Julian and two other family members eight days earlier in a mysterious crash of a private plane and desperately wanted to win in honor of his father's memory.

And it looked like that's exactly what would happen. By lap 178 of the 200-lap event, Martin led teammate Jeff Burton by 1.81 seconds, with Gordon back in fourth. But the third and final caution flag of the race flew one lap later, when Burton's brother Ward lost an engine in his Pontiac, dumping oil on the track.

When the leaders pitted, most took two tires. Jeff Burton was penalized because of loose lug nuts, and when the green flag flew on lap 185, Martin was first, followed by Dale Jarrett and Gordon, who had his crew pull out a right rear spring rubber and change two tires in just 9.2 seconds.

Gordon dispatched Jarrett on lap 189 and got by Martin two laps later after a couple of aborted attempts and drove to victory, while Martin faded to fourth. "When Ray called for two tires, I wasn't so sure about it," Gordon said after the race. "That thing just came to life, at least for 17 laps it did. I don't know what would have happened if we'd had to go much further. I couldn't believe it."

Neither could Martin, who had been dominant all afternoon. And it especially raised the suspicions of Roush, furious that for the fourth straight week Gordon's Chevrolet had won and one of Roush's Fords hadn't.

"It's pretty disappointing," said an emotionally distraught Martin. "I would have liked to have won this race. I don't care if I'd ever won another one, but I couldn't beat those guys. We gave it our best. We raced hard all day. It wasn't meant to be. It was almost a storybook ending."

Though Martin would stop Gordon's four-race winning streak six days later at Bristol Motor Speedway, earning the victory he wanted so much for his father, Roush didn't believe Gordon's success was by superior driving skill or mechanical preparation. Instead, he was certain Gordon and Evernham were cheating.

"Jeff Gordon is not a better race car driver than Mark Martin, and Ray Evernham is not a better crew chief than Jimmy Fennig," Roush said. "I'm just trying to figure out what's going on, because I'm missing something."

But Roush thought he figured it out when the Winston Cup teams traveled north for the August 30 Farm Aid on CMT 300 at New Hampshire International Speedway. At that race, Gordon again took two tires in a late-race pit stop yet managed to hold off Martin and others who took four and cruise to victory.

After the race, Roush and Evernham engaged in a shouting match in the garage, with Roush accusing Evernham of cheating by somehow doctoring the tires to improve performance. "It's the air, Jack," Evernham snapped back at Roush, saying, in effect, that the Hendrick team did a better job of managing air pressure in the tires than Roush's team did. Given that a change of half a pound of air pressure one way or another can radically alter a car's performance, keeping accurate track of it is one of the most important details a team must monitor during the race.

Roush didn't buy it. Instead, he claimed to have received a package in the mail from a company he did business with. It contained a can and a bottle, both marked "Tire Softener. Undetectable," along with a letter that said, "your competition is using it," though it did not specifically mention who.

"It made me mad more than anything else, because now I was faced with it," Roush said after receiving the letter and samples. "I could have my suspicions and I could be disgruntled, but I've got something now, and what am I going to do with it? Am I going to give it to my guys and ask them if they want to use it? I won't say that I didn't think about that. It crossed my mind."

Instead, on the morning of the New Hampshire race, Roush took the letter and the sample to the NASCAR trailer, where he turned them over to Mike Helton, then NASCAR's vice president for competition.

After the New Hampshire race, NASCAR confiscated Gordon's tires and Martin's as well, with tires from both teams being sent to independent laboratories for analysis. Ultimately they found nothing; no illegal substances of any kind.

Roush had claimed that Evernham was using an illegal and undetectable substance to "soak" or soften Gordon's tires. Such substances, which are legal in some forms of racing, work by heating up the rubber and softening the tires substantially. They were very popular in qualifying races during the 1960s, when NASCAR tire wars between Goodyear and Firestone were at their height.

The advantage of tire softeners is that they give vastly improved grip—but only for a couple of laps. Use a tire-soaking compound, and you might pick up two-tenths of a second for five laps, and then lose half a second a lap over the next 50.

As with equally illegal fuel additives, tire-soaking compounds are both strictly forbidden and readily available.

"There's guys out there, they're like drug dealers," said veteran Winston Cup competitor Ricky Rudd. "They're like, 'Here, I've got this for ya, I've got that for ya. I know you guys are having trouble qualifying. Put this on your tires, soak your tires with this stuff and I guarantee you'll win a pole.'"

"Somebody will come out with a new product, and it's usually just snake oil," added car owner Robert Yates. "And these salesmen have always [claimed to have] come from the shop that just won the last race. They are so full of bullshit."

"I know some Winston Cup teams use our products," said Johnny James, general manager of Winston-Salem, North

Carolina–based Pro-Blend Chemical Company, in a 2000 interview with Florida's *St. Petersburg Times*. "They use the legal ones, and they use some of the illegal ones. I don't know who, when, and how they get it in and make it work. But we know that they do. If they get caught, they knew whether it was legal or illegal."

"It's a free enterprise," James said of his business, which makes among other things, horsepower-boosting fuel additives and compounds to treat tires. "NASCAR can't come to us and say you can't sell to Jack Roush or Hendrick when we have no control over who buys it."

And while NASCAR frets about such vendors, in reality there's little, if anything, they can do about it.

"It seems like there is a growing number of outside sources who are making claims to team owners and crew members that they can come up with something that circumvents NASCAR's rules in the garage area," said NASCAR's Helton. "That is a concern to NASCAR, and if there is any way to react to that beyond the garage area, we're very interested in the ability to do that. The dilemma we've got is that our authority is basically limited to NASCAR members," he said.

For teams approached about using such substances, the temptations can be great. Of course, so are the potential penalties.

"You've got car owners in this garage area that how well they run determines if their sponsor comes back next year," Rudd said. "They've got to be thinking, 'If I get caught it's only 50 grand. If I don't look good and I don't run good, then I'm going to lose an $8 million-, $12 million-a-year sponsor.' So they're juggling $50,000 [against] $12 million. It's going to put guys in a position to have to cheat if the penalty's not heavy enough."

As far as Tiregate goes, however, no wrongdoing was ever discovered—and few minds were changed. Roush continued to insist that Evernham and Company were engaged in some form of skullduggery—after all, the team was sponsored by DuPont, one of the world's foremost chemical companies— while others said tire-soaking compounds don't work anyway and Roush was a crank and a sore loser.

One of the most interesting observations on the Tiregate saga came from Bickford.

"The reality is that tire soaking has been going on in Winston Cup and other forms of racing for years and years and years. But anybody who soaks tires will tell you that it's really a momentary thing," Bickford said. "You put a chemical in a tire, heat it up to 190 or 200 degrees, it dissipates most of those chemicals and they go away rapidly.

"If you go back and look at Jeff, he was never fast at the beginning of the runs, he was always fast at the end of the runs. Any crew chiefs who have any knowledge about the car at all, it's all about tire-wear consumption and the amount of heat you put into your tires to achieve what you want to achieve."

Bickford also said paying meticulous attention to details separates the great teams from the merely good ones. It's something he did when he was building Gordon's cars as a youth and something Evernham was famous for.

"One thing you can do is make sure that your wheels are round and straight. Because your wheels might not necessarily be round and straight, they could have been bumped, banged. Racing is about tolerances. If I want to be faster than you, and you work to 1/16 of an inch tolerance, and I work to 1/32, I will be faster, because I'm going to be a little bit closer in everything I do.

"The guys that win are all about elementary things: basics, basics, basics. Ray'll tell you it's Racing 101. It's not Winston Cup, it's Racing 101 applied. It's taking the wheels that everybody runs and selecting the wheels that run the truest. If your wheels that you buy have 0.30-inch total indicated runout, but I select wheels that have 0.15 total indicated runout [side-to-side movement] and I check my wheels every race for .015 runout and you assume that your wheel is right. If you assume, but I measure, I'll beat you every time. Consistently, not every race, but over time I will beat you. And when you're talking about Winston Cup racing, what is it? Consistency over time."

And it's not as if Gordon's car hadn't been scrutinized over the course of the season, either. After a particularly intensive post-race inspection at Pocono in July, Triplett noted that Gordon and Evernham had to take the Rainbow-colored No. 24 "home in a bucket" because it had been so thoroughly dismantled.

"There were rumors that some guys had pumps in the roll cages, where they pumped mercury from one side of the car to the other," explained Bickford. "You have to have a certain amount of left-side weight and a certain amount of right-side weight, and you pump all the weight from the right side of the car to the left side of the car and you pump it back over when you come back in. This is what they were hunting for with Ray. They thought he had sliding weights in his car. They drilled the frame full of holes hunting for moving weight boxes. It was enough work that the NASCAR officials prayed Jeff wouldn't win because of the amount of work that they would have to do after the event."

Ultimately, Tiregate came to a head at Darlington, during the first weekend of September. It was there, in the suffocating South Carolina heat of Labor Day weekend that Gordon was running for an unprecedented fourth straight Southern 500 victory.

NASCAR changed its process of distributing tires, waiting until just before the race to give them out to teams. They also confiscated tires after the race and put the top six finishers in the race on a chassis dyno to measure horsepower.

At Darlington, Winston Cup Director Gary Nelson said the seized New Hampshire tires that had come up clean in the first round of tests were being examined in even more painstaking detail. "What we're doing now is going as far as a DNA-type test on the tires. We are reverse-engineering the tires in a laboratory. We're taking it right back to the rubber tree to see what is in these tires and what amounts."

Roush was unconvinced. "I would like to think the No. 24 is not soaking their tires, but there is something really incredible going on with regard to the way they are able to do these miraculous late-race recoveries."

Naturally, Evernham didn't see it that way. "The way they treat this race team, it really pisses me off," he said after Gordon's New Hampshire win. "Jack needs to watch the tape and pay attention. It disgusts me that a grown man who is supposed to be intelligent isn't paying attention. I think it is a statement about how big his ego is. If somebody said the only reason you can beat them is to cheat, what would you think? It sounds to me like Jack is losing his mind."

Bickford said the whole fiasco may simply have been a case of others refusing to accept how good Evernham really was.

"I think it's the guys that can almost win. Those are the guys who are always pointing their fingers, because human nature, the male ego, requires that we have a reason why we've not achieved the same thing the other guy has," said Bickford.

"People say, 'I'm just as smart as Ray Evernham.' The fact that he won 49 races people ignore. They say 'He has more money, he was cheating more, he did this, nobody paid any attention. Jeff Gordon's the golden-haired boy, yada, yada, yada.' The fact that Ray Evernham worked 90 hours a week and read hundreds of books and studied every single thing and he was consistently a winner from the time he was a kid, and he had a kid drive for him who was consistently a winner and every guy on his team was a consistent winner in everything they did, that doesn't have anything to do with it."

The Tiregate probe officially ended with a press conference September 11 at Richmond International Raceway, where NASCAR and Goodyear officials announced that yet another set of independent tests had found nothing. Case closed.

"There have been some insinuations that I am a sore loser, that I'm just frustrated and that I am just banging out aimlessly in space because I am frustrated with being defeated as many times as we have been and it does hurt me a lot,"

Roush said after Darlington. "It hurts me as much as anybody I can imagine being hurt, to try as hard as we do and to come up empty as much as we do, but we've got to be adults about this thing."

The following summer Roush would be back in the center of another rules fight with NASCAR, only this time one of his teams was the accused.

The latest controversy involved Greg Biffle, who drove for Roush in the NASCAR Craftsman Truck Series, the sport's AA division. In his rookie season, Biffle won nine of the first 22 Craftsman Truck Series races of 1999. His ninth victory came September 24 at Las Vegas Motor Speedway, where he fought off former series champion Jack Sprague, who drove for Hendrick Motorsports, Roush's most bitter rival in the Winston Cup Series.

The win pushed Biffle's points lead to 130 over Sprague, an almost insurmountable margin, with just three races to go in the season. But two hours after the race was completed, truck series Director Wayne Auton announced that an "unapproved" intake manifold had been found on Biffle's truck.

In NASCAR vernacular, that means a specific part—in this case an intake manifold—had not been approved for use in competition in writing by NASCAR. The part in question must carry a specific ID number and conform to NASCAR's dimensions, specifications, and material composition.

As in the Martin case nine years earlier, the resulting penalties would cost the team the title. Biffle was docked 120 points, the difference between finishing first and last in the 36-truck field, and his crew chief, Randy Goss, was fined $48,860. Biffle's penalty knocked all but 10 points off his lead over Sprague.

The fine and penalty stunned team owner Roush. "That intake manifold was prepared last winter. It was presented to NASCAR at the first race, and this is the fourth time it's been raced this year," Roush said after the fine was announced. Roush contended the manifold had been approved; NASCAR in turn asserted that the manifold's internal passageways had been modified beyond legal limits, allowing improved airflow and more horsepower.

During a teleconference five days after the race, team owner Roush and team President Geoff Smith announced that they were planning to appeal the ruling and claimed they had overwhelming documentation that NASCAR had, in fact, previously approved the part, which had been raced more than a dozen times on the team's two trucks.

Then it got personal, with the integrity of the official, who NASCAR declined to identify, called into question. Roush and Smith both claimed the manifold went through inspection on numerous occasions without a problem. But after Las Vegas, Roush contended, a NASCAR inspector changed his story about letting the manifold pass tech inspection at earlier races.

"Said Roush: "To have somebody come back later and say they hadn't seen [a part], or it wasn't like that when they saw it, in order to apparently be able to sidestep some potential criticism for whether they made a sound, subjective decision is really an uncertainty that would just make life unbearable."

And unbearable is exactly what life was for the team. Despite reams of evidence to the contrary from Roush about the manifold, the National Stock Car Racing Commission upheld NASCAR's ruling October 5, just as they had upheld NASCAR's penalties to Roush's Winston Cup team more than nine years earlier. Roush, understandably, was livid. "Whenever somebody comes through the NASCAR gates as a competitor, all the rights to the classic Western civilization judicial system, you give up," Roush said.

When asked about the potential impact of the ruling on Biffle's title hopes, Roush said bitterly, "I don't care about championships anymore. This is bigger than that."

Sprague ultimately went on to claim the 1999 Craftsman Truck Series by a mere eight points, despite scoring just three wins to Biffle's nine and scoring an equal number of top-10 finishes. Over the course of a 25-race season, eight points is equal to the difference of finishing 10th instead of 12th in a single race. Or to state it another way, it's less than two-tenths of 1 percent.

Of course, not everyone was sympathetic to Roush's plight. "I don't care if you ran the thing 100 times before you get caught," said Bickford of Biffle's manifold. "I don't care if you were speeding down I-85 every single day for the last 10 years, when you got your speeding ticket, you were illegal. I don't care if Biffle ran his intake manifold for three seasons, if it's wrong, it's wrong. Same with Jeff Gordon."

Dale Earnhardt's Richard Childress Racing Chevrolet gets a careful check from NASCAR inspectors at Talladega in April 2000. That controversial weekend, it was one of many cars to have bodywork that NASCAR officials ordered changed. (Sam Sharpe)

Chapter 8

I don't think it's real out of character for Talladega or Daytona to have a lot of cars have to do some work. Competitors push the edge here, push the edge there. We try and get 'em back on the other side.

—Kevin Triplett, NASCAR operations director

Talladega 2000
Running Wild

O n the morning of April 14, 2000, at Talladega Superspeedway, the first in a series of events began to unfold that would again plunge NASCAR into a nationally debated cheating controversy.

By 9 a.m., the weather was raw and cold, the kind of day competitors were used to at places like New Hampshire and Pocono, but almost never in Alabama. A hard, steady rain was falling all around the mammoth 2.66-mile track, a storm that was a potential recipe for disaster for the 48 Winston Cup teams entered to compete in the Diehard 500 April 16.

Crew chiefs and mechanics spend untold hours dreaming up and then creating devices to circumvent the rules for restrictor-plate racetracks, while NASCAR officials are constantly trying to uncover them. Think of it as a high-stakes poker game with a purse of $2.9 million at this race, plus up to 185 Winston Cup points. And make no mistake about, it's a zero-sum game: At every race, one team wins, everyone else goes home a loser.

And that's why so many people are willing to push the rules to the limit, or at least try.

The weather washed out morning practice, which meant inspectors had all the time they wanted to go over every car with a fine-tooth comb. Inspection ran all day instead of a couple of hours, and by the time it was completed, fully 43 of 48 cars flunked, instead of the usual three or four. The violations unearthed by NASCAR were all over the board, so broad and comprehensive that Gary Nelson hosted an impromptu press conference to discuss them.

When asked where most of the infractions occurred, Nelson laughed out loud. "It's a little bit of everything," he says. "Front, back, middle, top, bottom." And why were parts seized? "About any reason," said Nelson. "Too small, too wide, too skinny, too tall, too short, whatever the limits are. Many of the parts are just beyond those limits."

One of the cars that had the toughest battle with inspectors was the black No. 3 Chevrolet owned by Richard Childress and driven by seven-time NASCAR Winston Cup champion Dale Earnhardt, winner of both Talladega races in 1999.

NASCAR inspectors ordered the rear-end bodywork cut completely off the No. 3, claiming the rear fascia was an experimental, unapproved part. On a production car, the rear fascia would be loosely defined as the back end of the car, the place where you'd find the rear bumper, taillights, and trunk opening. On a Winston Cup car, these individual components are replaced with the one-piece fascia, which is made of composite plastics.

Nearby, in the pit of defending Winston Cup champion Dale Jarrett, crew chief Todd Parrott was forced to make similar, though less extensive, repairs on Jarrett's No. 88 Ford, which didn't fit NASCAR's rear-end templates. When asked about what NASCAR ordered him to do, Parrott barked, "Fix it." He didn't elaborate, but he made his displeasure abundantly clear to anyone nearby.

Not everyone took it so seriously. Michael "Fatback" McSwain, who was the crew chief for Jarrett's teammate Ricky Rudd, just shrugged when asked about what he'd been ordered to do to allow Rudd's car to pass inspection. "No big deal," he said.

At a low-speed track where aerodynamics play little role in a car's performance, such as Martinsville or Bristol, NASCAR might choose at random half a dozen body templates to check the cars, just to make sure no team is too flagrant in its "customizing." In an ordinary weekend at Talladega, NASCAR might use 12 to 15 templates, because teams massage the bodywork here in an attempt to minimize aerodynamic drag and make the cars faster.

The rain that was falling on Talledega that Friday was a luxury for the inspectors; it gave them time to use virtually every single template on every car. The result was a rash of minor violations, most involving contours around the base of the windshield or the base of the C pillars at the back end of the roof. You could spot who was caught doing what by the patches of body filler and primer where they had to make hasty fixes. By race time, those repairs would be freshly painted and undetectable to race fans.

While crewmen feverishly worked with pop rivets and Bondo to repair Earnhardt's black No. 3 Chevrolet in time for qualifying, car owner Childress was philosophical.

"They just didn't like the way we had it fixed up," Childress said of the NASCAR inspectors. "We did everything we could to get as much drag out of the car as we could, and the way we did it they just didn't like it. It's our job to do it and their job to tell us that we can't." What he didn't disclose is that the rear fascia his crew members removed from Earnhardt's car was replaced by an identical part, one of the oldest tricks in the racer's book. NASCAR officials, satisfied that they had forced the RCR team to remove the offending fascia, assumed the replacement part attached to the black No. 3 was different than the old one. It wasn't, but no one told the inspectors that. It wouldn't be until months later in a sit-down interview that Childress revealed what his crew did. His feeling was that the first fascia was legal and unfairly ordered to be removed, so why not replace it with another legal one?

And if Childress seemed relatively unfazed at Talladega, there were no hard feelings from the NASCAR side or other competitors, either.

"Most of 'em are taking it pretty well," Nelson said of the cars that flunked inspections. "You know, 'Well, we thought we'd try it. It didn't work, so we'll go back.' Some of them were prepared with parts to switch out."

"I don't think it's real out of character for Talladega or Daytona to have a lot of cars have to do some work," said Kevin Triplett. "Competitors push the edge here, push the edge there. We try and get 'em back on the other side.

"If you're a basketball player and you're down inside in the paint, you're going to hold the guy's jersey to try and keep him from getting a move on you. You're not supposed to do that, but you do. It's just the nature of being competitive and trying to be better than the guy beside you," Triplett explained.

"What we've got to do is try to make sure that everybody in the garage is dealing with the same deck of cards. And if we make everybody make the same changes, we feel like we're doing it."

But Friday was only the beginning of one of the strangest weekends—and one of the dirtiest, at least in terms of rules violations—anyone could remember.

Most of the cars entered at Talladega had to make body-work modifications. Some of the modifications, like those on the cars of Earnhardt and teammate Mike Skinner, were extensive and took several hours to complete; others could be fixed in a few minutes—the old Junior Johnson philosophy of "make it wrong, but make it easy to put right."

Outside the NASCAR trailer in the Winston Cup garage on Saturday morning, there was quite a collection of unapproved parts, and others that were blatantly illegal.

Lightweight fuel cells made from too-thin metal were confiscated from the cars of Jerry Nadeau, Mark Martin, Ted Musgrave, Sterling Marlin, and Matt Kenseth. Scott Pruett's Ford had its carburetor taken; unapproved rear-wheel hubs were grabbed from the cars of Martin and Elliott Sadler; Marlin's Chevrolet was minus a set of rear springs; and the rear spoilers of three of Roush Racing's five Fords were taken by NASCAR inspectors.

The Roush rear spoilers were a particular source of fascination in the NASCAR trailer. The approved rear spoilers on Winston Cup Fords are supposed to have a gentle curve or arc, almost like the blade of a hockey stick. One of Roush's was bent at sharp angles in half a dozen places and looked almost like a boomerang, in an apparent attempt to reduce drag.

When asked what was wrong with one of the spoilers, an official threw his hands up in the air. "It's just wrong, look at it!" he shouted. "Everything about it is wrong. It's just, just *wrong*." Then he grew quiet for a second and said simply, "Look this thing is fucked up, OK? But I can't say that. Let's just leave it at 'wrong.'" The reason the official was upset was that this particular spoiler was so egregiously flagrant in its illegality that NASCAR took it as an insult to their collective intelligence that a team would try something so ham-fisted. Despite, or maybe because of, the cops and robbers nature of their work, inspectors grudgingly respect creative and innovative attempts to beat their laws. They have no patience, however, for amateurish jobs like this clearly bogus spoiler, regarding it as a waste of everyone's time when there's more important work to be done.

A few minutes after the episode in the NASCAR trailer, car owner Jack Roush held court in the Talladega Infield Media Center and admitted that, unbeknownst to him, several of his crew chiefs have pushed the rules beyond the limit.

"The [No.] 17, 97, and the 16 were all snared by NASCAR's spoiler-checking process," Roush said patiently. "Some of the teams think they understand how NASCAR is going to tech something, and they come back and prepare for that. Those cars, without my knowledge, had taken some liberties in the spoiler area. NASCAR took those, and I support and applaud that. I'll have conversations with all the crew chiefs that what they did was ill-advised."

But the final question of the press conference sent Roush on an angry rant. He was asked by a reporter about the incident ten years earlier in Richmond, when Mark Martin was penalized for an intake manifold spacer violation that ultimately cost him the championship (and, of course, Greg Biffle lost his truck series championship in 1999 in a similar dispute).

"I'm used to winning. I've won lots of championships [in other forms of racing]," said Roush, his voice choking back emotion. "I don't know if I'll ever win a NASCAR championship. I almost don't care. I feel as bad about the 1990 thing and what happened at Richmond today as I did then. And I don't feel any less bad about what happened in the truck deal.

"The luster is way off of NASCAR's championships," said Roush. "In the meantime, we're going to be in their face. We're going to win as many races as we can . . . and whether I win a NASCAR championship or not is not a major concern. My heart's broke."

Later that afternoon, Joe Nemechek won the Talladega Busch Series race. Afterward, Nemechek's car was found to have a left rear quarter panel that was too low, the third time his team had been caught breaking the rules in the last two years. His crew chief, Brian Pattie was later fined $20,000.

This time, Nemechek claimed he did nothing wrong and said the low quarter panel may have been the result of contact with another car on the track.

But earlier in the year, when his pole-winning time was disallowed for the Daytona Busch race, he had been a little more forthright. "As a competitor, you're always trying to do as much as you can do to get every advantage you can get," he said.

Whether or not Nemechek's Talladega infraction came about purely by accident or as the result of pushing the envelope, it was the first of several big incidents. Over the next three weeks, a series of events unfolded that threw the garage into an uproar and called into question the integrity of the sport and some of its key participants.

On Sunday, April 16, Jeff Gordon ended a 13-race non-winning streak to claim victory in the DieHard 500, the kind of typical knuckle-biter of a race Talladega is known for.

Pole-sitter Jeremy Mayfield faded to 14th and was never much of a factor in the race. But within a couple of days, rumors started making the rounds that NASCAR had detected an illegal substance in Mayfield's fuel during a routine check late in the race. As days passed, speculation and rumors heightened. NASCAR acknowledged an investigation was underway, but declined official comment.

Rumors and conspiracy theories ran wild, especially on the Internet, a haven for so much paranoid innuendo it makes Kennedy assassination conspiracy buffs seem well grounded and in the know. Some suggested that NASCAR was delaying acting on Mayfield's illegal fuel until after the running of the NAPA Auto Parts 500 at California Speedway on April 30. The conspiracy theorists detailed a compelling argument: California Speedway was built by Roger Penske, co-owner of Mayfield's car. In mid-1999, Penske sold his raceway empire for $740 million to International Speedway Corporation, which is majority-owned by NASCAR President Bill France and his family. After the deal closed, Penske was named vice chairman of ISC.

When the Mayfield brouhaha came up, France didn't want to embarrass Penske, the conspiracy theorists argued, so NASCAR waited until after the race to rule on the fuel, an assertion Helton would strongly refute later on.

Sponsorship issues clouded the storyline even further. Mayfield's team was backed by Mobil 1 motor oil, in what was rumored to be one of NASCAR's most lucrative sponsorship packages, purportedly in excess of $10 million annually. And the deal was in its final year.

When the Winston Cup traveling circus arrived in California for the following race, the already bizarre atmosphere took a further twist. For the second time in a row, the support race on Saturday was won by a Winston Cup regular. This time Johnny Benson claimed victory in the Winston West Series, sort of a West Coast version of NASCAR's Busch Series.

And for the second time in a row, the winner was caught cheating. Benson's Tyler Jet Motorsports Pontiac was found to have an unapproved intake manifold. Like Nemechek at Talladega, Benson got to keep the victory. But crew chief James Ince was fined $10,440, and the team lost 108 points.

Astonishingly, the next day Mayfield won the NAPA Auto Parts 500, his first victory in almost two full years and only his second in 187 career Winston Cup races. Even more astonishingly, his car flunked post-race tech inspection when it was determined to be too low, which Mayfield claimed was the result of him jumping on the car in victory lane after the race.

About the alleged fuel additive NASCAR detected at Talladega, Mayfield was defiant in victory at California. "Didn't use nothing, didn't need nothing," he said.

But the truth was a bit more complicated.

Finally, on May 2, Helton spelled out NASCAR's findings and the subsequent penalties.

NASCAR discovered an illegal over-the-counter fuel additive had been slipped into Mayfield's fuel by one of his Penske-Kranefuss Racing crewmen, who NASCAR insisted acted alone and without the knowledge of anyone else on the team.

The additive was what's known as an oxygenate, designed to increase the oxygen content of gasoline and therefore increase horsepower. "It's called 1, 4-dioxane," Helton said. "It is something that's available fairly readily in high-performance shops and motorcycle shops in particular. It's something you can go buy off the shelf."

There are three cardinal sins in NASCAR: tampering with fuel, tires, or engine size. And Mayfield's team got caught violating one of them. "It's a very sacred area," Helton said. "Anything that works against us in that area we're very sensitive to."

Predictably, the punishment was severe: Mayfield was docked 151 driver points, which knocked him from seventh to 14th in the standings; car owner Michael Kranefuss was docked 151 car owner points and fined $50,000; crew chief Peter Sospenzo was suspended until June 6.

In the old days it had been a lot easier to deal with such transgressions, usually behind closed doors, when the sport was small, regional, and lacking a national TV contract and Fortune 500 sponsors. Now that it's in the public eye, NASCAR has had to step up its enforcement efforts dramatically. "NASCAR, and particularly the NASCAR Winston Cup Series, is not the same as it was two, three, four, five, or certainly 10 years ago," Helton said in assessing the penalties. "The magnitude of the sport, the status of the sport, the involvement by teams and sponsors and tracks and fans fortunately has grown. Along with that growth comes a great deal more responsibility, and particularly from NASCAR's perspective the core of our business—what goes on in that garage area—is more sensitive and more keen today than it ever has been in order to live up to this growth.

"NASCAR works very hard with 60-some officials every weekend and nearly 30 templates and then 112 different steps and procedures of inspection to keep that community all intact. In the year 2000, the season so far, we've taken over 500 fuel samples throughout the course of the current season. This is the first one that we've had not come back correctly. So when that occurred, it was the responsibility of NASCAR to act as fairly and correctly as possible," Helton said.

Helton said the delayed response was not the result of politics but because NASCAR sent the tainted fuel to multiple independent laboratories for analysis. "In today's world, when we come back with a big penalty, we need to be exact," he said. "We used multiple laboratories to confirm the fact that there was something in the fuel that didn't belong."

In discussing the penalty, Helton also added perhaps the only moment of levity while explaining why the penalty was 151 points, 25 points more than the 126 Mayfield earned with his finish at Talladega.

"I relate it to when you were young and your father pulled off his belt—at least when I was young, that's the way it was done—the first two whacks were for what I did, and the last one was so I wouldn't do it again," said Helton.

Two days later, Sospenzo was fined $25,000 for the roof height violation at California, though no points were taken away.

Sospenzo would later hint that he couldn't rule out sabotage, possibly from a rogue Penske crewman or someone from another team as the source of the tainted fuel sample. "It definitely makes you think a little bit more about who your friends are and who aren't your friends," he said.

While Sospenzo said he had no knowledge of how the additive got in the gas and said he had never been in trouble with NASCAR before, he admitted, "There isn't a crew chief in this garage who hasn't pushed the envelope to the limit. But sometimes you just fall off on the wrong side."

In the end, the entire controversy drew criticism from all sides. Competitors, who tend to be extremely cautious about what they say for fear of invoking NASCAR's wrath, were reticent, while the racing media skewered the sanctioning body.

Some thought Mayfield or his team should have been suspended prior to California; others thought at the very least he should have been disciplined before the race.

"We're playing by NASCAR's rules, and we're going to race by them and stand by them," said Jimmy Makar, crew chief on Bobby Labonte's car, which finished second to Mayfield at California. Makar was angry that Mayfield was allowed to race, but knew that decision was NASCAR's alone. To speculate about what the proper penalty ought to be would be pointless, Makar said. "That car was allowed to race this weekend and that's just the way it is. Woulda, shoulda, coulda, goes a long way, but that's not the way it was."

"I don't think the win will sit real well," added car owner Bill Davis.

"Hey, cheating's cheating," said Todd Parrott, crew of 1999 champion Jarrett's team. "If you get caught, you've got to get penalized for it."

"There isn't a whole lot you can say under the circumstances," admitted car owner Kranefuss. "Mistakes were made, and there were certainly some grave errors in judgment. Needless to say we accept the penalty, we have taken disciplinary action within our team, and we apologize to our fans, our sponsors, NASCAR, and the other teams."

Then, Kranefuss made an astonishing admission. "One day maybe we can talk about what really happened, and you guys hopefully will understand a little better," he said. "If you one day hear what the real story is and you hear about how naive and amateurish the whole deal had come together, you would not doubt it."

But the furtive nature of the discussion only served to stoke the already-raging fires of cynicism in the Winston Cup garage.

"The story of all the incredible, grand, glorious, heart-warming coincidences associated with major league stock-car racing would shame the writers of Grimm's Fairy Tales. Norman Rockwell couldn't have captured them on canvas," wrote Monte Dutton of the *Gastonia* [North Carolina] *Gazette*.

Others suggested that Mayfield shouldn't even have been allowed to race at California. And the suspicion, paranoia, and frayed nerves caused by this incident had everybody second-guessing NASCAR and wondering what really happened.

David Poole of the *Charlotte Observer* weighed in: "They might as well start calling the place NASCAR parks its red and white truck at the track each weekend Area 51. That's the atmosphere in Winston Cup racing these days. Nothing is taken at face value. Every action and every reaction by stock-car racing's governing body is met with skepticism. Every decision is considered part of a grand conspiracy."

The competitors in the garage were also the objects of conspiracy theories. Maybe the team—or at least a high-ranking team member—believed the illegal substance would not be detected during inspection. That had been the argument in Tiregate two years earlier, when conspiracy theorists believed Jeff Gordon's tires were treated with an undetectable performance enhancer, perhaps developed by his sponsor, DuPont. Mayfield's car was caught with doctored fuel and was sponsored by a petroleum company.

Was this a coincidence, or could Mayfield's situation have been the result of another problem such as an act of sabotage by a disgruntled or rival crew member? Maybe. Another theory floated was that it was an act of simple stupidity by a team member. The illegal substance was found in the team's catch can, the device a crew member plugs into the overflow vent on the rear fascia during refueling to catch excess gas. Maybe a crewman had dumped something in the catch can as he was cleaning up around the pit box at the end of the race, forgetting that it would be collected and inspected.

Maybe this was just one of the situations where an innocent mistake turned out to have devastating consequences on an entire team and the careers of the people in it. Maybe it was sinister, maybe it was stupid, maybe the team was just a bunch of cheatin' sumbitches who got caught and punished as deserved. But no matter how you dissect it, the price was a high one to pay for everyone.

Ultimately, the entire incident tore the team apart. Team co-owner Penske, who is fiercely protective of his reputation, was publicly humiliated by the controversy. Before the year was out, Kranefuss, the former head of Ford's worldwide racing operations, sold his ownership interest to Penske and struck off on his own to start a team with driver Shawna Robinson in the minor-league ARCA series. By mid-2001, Mayfield was gone, too, fired in an acrimonious departure, despite winning a race earlier in the season. At the end of 2001, Mobil departed as a primary sponsor, and the team shut down for good. Sospenzo spent 2002 on the sidelines, reportedly still drawing a salary from the team, but for the first half of the season at least, out of the sport.

So what really happened? To this day, the topic is sensitive. Most sources in the garage not only declined to speak on the record or off, but even went so far as to say that they didn't want to be asked about it or have their names mentioned in connection with the team. Even crew members on other teams didn't want to talk about it. One reason that this sensitivity persists is that no one wants to risk being perceived as the one "who ratted out" the 12 team when so many details remain murky.

One former team member, who spoke on condition of strict anonymity, said the crewman who put the illegal fuel additive in was told do so "by a higher-up." This effectively dismisses the popular garage speculation that the action was, in effect, a wild-hair sort of idea by a renegade crewman. The fuel was discovered, apparently, when another team reported it to NASCAR.

Still, it's hard to imagine a team as good as Penske-Kranefuss flagrantly cheating in one of NASCAR's most sensitive areas. Everyone knows random fuel checks are part of the race, especially at a place like Talladega where horse-power is at a premium and cars undergo unusually high degrees of scrutiny. It simply doesn't make sense that they'd try something that bone-headed and obvious. Clearly, Mayfield's car didn't have an appreciable performance advantage or run any better after the last pit stop.

In this specific case, the risk-reward ratio was way out of whack on the side of risk. Mayfield was a contender week in and week out, so his team presumably didn't need to cheat to run competitively. Conversely, the penalties for getting caught turned out to be huge. It's damn hard to conceive of a top-10 team risking so much with so little to gain. Not impossible, but hard to believe.

To its credit, NASCAR did what it had to do, whatever the underlying cause of the infraction. And for the remainder of the season, the sanctioning body continued to send out strong messages about not condoning cheating.

When the Winston Cup circuit arrived in Sonoma, California, for the Save Mart/Kragen 350 in June 2000, Rusty Wallace put his Penske Racing South Ford on the pole, with a lap that was half a second faster than anyone else in the field. It was Wallace's sixth pole in just 16 races. In a sport where qualifying spots are usually separated by a few thousandths or maybe one or two hundredths of a second, for one car to be half a second faster than everyone else is unusual, even on a road course.

Wallace was also the teammate to Jeremy Mayfield, which meant other teams were probably quietly lobbying NASCAR to give Wallace's car a little extra attention in inspection.

After Wallace won the pole at Sonoma, rumors immediately began about the car's legality. General Motors racing executives in attendance began whispering off the record to reporters that Wallace's car was using pistons, connecting rods, and a crankshaft made of a space-age lightweight alloy that supposedly was 68 percent beryllium and 32 percent aluminum. If that were true, the lighter engine components, in theory, would allow the engine to spin faster internally and produce more power.

According to the GM people the high-tech alloy was developed in England at a Penske subsidiary, Ilmor Engineering, which builds engines for the McLaren-Mercedes Formula One team in Europe and had built engines for Chevrolet and Mercedes in the CART FedEx Championship Series here in the United States. Of course, given the politics and innuendo and gossip-mongering that goes on in the modern Winston Cup garage, all of this could have been completely true, or it could just as easily have been a total fabrication dreamed up over a couple of martinis on the flight from Detroit to San Francisco for the race. But either way, everyone was talking about it.

And then the unthinkable happened. To the utter horror of Wallace and his crew, the team's pole-winning engine was completely dismantled out in the open in the pits. While inspections are open in Winston Cup generally, this one was a shocking exception: For the first time in anyone's memory, NASCAR didn't simply measure engine displacement and cubic inches. Instead they totally stripped the engine of its guts, removing the highly secretive and proprietary internal components, including the custom-designed pistons, rods, crankshaft, and camshaft. Then the inspectors set the parts down on their workbench, naked in front of the entire garage area and the race teams.

Some teams photographed the inspection and the engine parts as they were put on the workbench; others sent team members in plain clothes to "watch" what was happening and scribble down notes. The inspection understandably enraged the Penske organization.

"It's the most obscene and unprofessional thing I've seen done in a long time," said a furious Wallace. "When a team works real, real hard to be the best and to work as hard as they do for an engine combination, that's totally unacceptable, to take every piece of the engine and lay it out for God and everybody to see. This is not something that's been done in the past."

While Wallace acknowledged that engine teardowns are part of the process, he added, "They [NASCAR] don't usually tear them down on an asphalt parking lot where every team member, every media person, every fan can take pictures and see. It was such a bad scene that it was almost nasty."

"I was disappointed in the way it was handled, that every-body got to write down whatever they saw," added Robin Pemberton, Wallace's crew chief. "I'm speechless. I'm really hurt by the whole thing. Never have they stripped [the engine] right down to the bare block. We're prepared to build engines in the shop and only take certain things off them at the racetrack. So we didn't have some of the special tools that it took. It was borderline barbaric."

As for NASCAR's response, Helton said, "All of our inspec-tion processes are open to the rest of the competitors. Always have been." Helton did, however, acknowledge that the inspections of the engines were a little bit more rigorous this time out for the cars of Wallace and Wally Dallenbach, the fastest second-round qualifier at Sears Point. "We did go a little bit further because of conversations in the garage area about exotic metals and different things," Helton said. "We took the pistons and the cranks out of them, which took maybe a little bit more time than we had in the past, but it's the same process we've always had."

Yes, it is. Win too much, run too fast, and teardowns and inspections will be living hells, even if you're legal—maybe *espe-cially* if you're legal—just as they were for Jeff Gordon in 1998 or Bill Elliott in 1985 or even Karl Kiekhaefer way back in 1955.

Then again, Gordon would have problems of his own just a couple of months later. When Gordon won the fall Richmond race in September, NASCAR officials announced afterwards that they "had issues" with the intake manifold on his Hendrick Motorsports Chevrolet.

The manifold taken off Gordon's car was made of magnesium, not aluminum. NASCAR considered it an unapproved part. The manifold was identical in casting to the aluminum ones, offering no horsepower advantage. The sole edge the magnesium manifold offered was that it was a couple of pounds lighter than its aluminum counterpart, which meant the crew could lower the car's center of gravity a little bit by adding an offsetting amount of ballast somewhere else in the car. The difference was small enough that it offered very little performance gain.

Still, NASCAR threw the book at Gordon, Hendrick, and crew chief Robbie Loomis, who had replaced Ray Evernham midway through the 1999 season. Gordon was fined 100 driver points, which ultimately would drop him from eighth to ninth in the season-ending Winston Cup standings. Hendrick was penalized 100 car owner points, and Loomis was slapped with a $25,000 fine. But what really shocked Gordon's fellow competitors was that some GM teams had been using the magnesium manifold since the Texas race, a full five months earlier, and most were running it at Richmond when Gordon won. In addition, the rule book didn't stipulate what material the manifold had to be built from. Hendrick Motorsports, armed with reams of supporting data and signed affidavits from GM officials, filed an appeal with the National Stock Car Racing Commission.

Despite the fact that such appeals have historically been unsuccessful, Hendrick and GM hoped for the best. And they had what they thought was a strong case. NASCAR inspector Jimmy Cox, one of Nelson's top lieutenants, had seen the magnesium manifold before it was used in competition and had informally given GM the OK to run it.

"We had shared it with NASCAR officials and at no time were we asked to submit it [for formal approval]," said Doug Duchardt, who headed the General Motors Winston Cup racing program. "We would never want to put our teams at risk like that. It's been inspected and torn down multiple times, and this time it was deemed inappropriate. We felt we were communicating it to the proper levels." The three-person NSCRC panel concluded that "all witnesses acknowledged that the approved NASCAR intake manifold is aluminum and that the magnesium manifold hadn't been formally submitted to NASCAR headquarters and was not approved by NASCAR."

"We really got screwed," said one high-ranking Hendrick team member, who claimed NASCAR was retaliating unfairly against the team. "Mike Helton even called Rick [Hendrick] and told him he was sorry about it, but he had to do it. Something like this could cost the team our sponsorship. We've all got morals and cheating clauses in our deals. We're lucky we didn't lose a sponsor over this."

But behind the public penalty and protest, the real story of the Gordon manifold was a simple screwup. At Darlington, one week before Richmond, GM officials met with their NASCAR counterparts to discuss upcoming rules changes in 2001 for the Busch Series. Specifically, in 2001, Busch teams would be allowed to run higher-horsepower engines very similar to those in Winston Cup, instead of the much-lower-horsepower V-8s they'd used historically.

During the meeting, GM officials asked Busch Series Director John Darby if they had any problem with GM cars using their Winston Cup magnesium intake manifold in the Busch Series in 2001. "What magnesium intake manifold?" Darby asked.

"The one we've been running since Texas," GM officials countered. At some point during the weekend, Darby broached the subject with Nelson and Helton, who said no such manifold had been formally approved. It was apparently decided at that point that NASCAR would penalize the next GM race winner that used the magnesium manifold. And although Bobby Labonte won the Darlington race, his Pontiac had the old aluminum manifold and therefore was not penalized. Gordon, however, was not so lucky a week later at Richmond.

As the 2000 season ended, NASCAR was on a roll: The sanctioning body enjoyed record attendance and popularity and announced a new, six-year $2.4 billion television contract with Fox and NBC that put the once regional sport of stock-car racing on a par with other major league sports. Behind the scenes, though, NASCAR was working harder than ever to keep a lid on the creativity of its competitors. It would need to, because the competitors were working harder, too.

After qualifying for the 2001 Daytona 500 ended, NASCAR seized one of each of the four competing manufacturers' fastest cars for wind-tunnel testing in Marietta, Ga. NASCAR took the cars of (from left) Tony Stewart, Rusty Wallace, Bill Elliott, and Dale Earnhardt to measure aerodynamic downforce and drag. (Tom Copeland)

Chapter 9

Twenty years ago, you didn't know if, when you went in inspection, it was going to be OK today and wrong next week.

—Larry McReynolds

Inspection/Daytona 2001
Restoring Order

Although Gary Nelson's rule-bending reputation got him his job as Winston Cup director, the way in which he has tightened up inspection and eliminated arbitrary interpretation may well prove to be his enduring legacy. By the time the teams arrived at Daytona in 2001, the process was much different than it was in prior decades.

"The biggest thing I see different in 2001 versus 1980 is that there are a lot more things being checked," said Larry McReynolds. "I'm not talking about a few things; I'm talking about hundreds of things. That's just NASCAR being smarter and gaining knowledge. The biggest thing they've done is put a fair amount of consistency in their inspection. A lot of cut and dry, black and white, red and green. Gary's done a really good job at taking the tape measure for the most part out of the inspectors' hands. No longer do you read a ruler to see if your roof height is 51 inches. You got a gauge that drops down; red means you're low, green means you're good. Same with the quarter-panel heights. Same even with the size of the rear spoiler. No longer does a guy view a tape measure. There's a template that fits the size of the rear spoiler. I think that's probably the biggest thing they've done that's good for the competitors. A lot of us bitch and moan and groan about the templates. And there are a lot of templates. But those templates let you go to the racetrack and know when you get there whether you are going to have a problem or not. Twenty years ago, you didn't know if, when you went in inspection, it was going to be OK today and wrong next week. When you go home at night and lay your head down, you know that you didn't get beat because somebody was an inch lower on their roof or because somebody's rear deck was pulled down an inch lower."

Prior to the 2001 Daytona 500, Nelson explained the current inspection process NASCAR uses on race weekends to ensure the legality of the competitors.

"The first thing, which a lot of people don't realize, is the cars are all unloaded off the trailers, and they go into a safety inspection. We have officials who have a checklist that check off all the safety items on the car. And that's about a five-hour process for 45 cars," Nelson explained. "Of 50 officials looking at the cars, 40 of those officials are going over safety items. We go through the whole garage, and then we go through safety items."

Among the safety items NASCAR checks closely are seat belts. Roll bars are measured to make sure the metal tubing conforms to minimum thickness rules, and other items like head-restraint nets are checked, too.

Once cars pass through the safety items, then the mechanical inspection begins. Nelson has at his disposal nearly 30 different precision-milled aluminum templates to measure the various external dimension of each race car. The cars must fit tolerances of just .060 of an inch or go back to make modifications.

Some of the templates are used at every race, most notably the so-called "long template" that runs from the nose of the car, lengthwise across the roof and trunk, ending up at the rear spoiler. This is the most important measuring device used in controlling the aerodynamic properties of the car.

But the number of other templates NASCAR inspectors use on a given weekend is a secret kept in Nelson's head until the last possible minute. After the safety inspection is concluded, "We begin with competition items. We put the templates on, we check the height of the car," said Nelson. "We start with templates—more than 25, more like 27 or 28. We'll start with templates, which are competition items and ensure what's fair and maintain a level playing field. At races like Daytona where we have a whole day for inspection, we use every template on every car. As we move away from Daytona and we move to the two- and three-day events, we decide which templates of the 28 we use. We might put 10 templates on at Rockingham next week. But we will not decide which 10 templates we'll put on until the morning we start. Our officials won't know—nobody will know—until the cars are already coming off the trailer. The decision is made as the cars are being unloaded so no official can be questioned as to, 'Well, you called so-and-so and told him what templates were going to be used.'" Nelson's secrecy helps prevent even the suggestion of collusion, which would be ruinous to the sport.

After the template checks, Nelson said, "We kind of shift gears into competition items, engine sizes, then we go into the size of the fuel lines and the things that would give a guy an edge competition-wise and we make sure that's fair. We level the field there, take away items that don't fit.

"After that it's practice. After practice ends, we go into qualifying inspection, which is a mixture of safety items and competition items. Every car is checked the same as the next car, so whatever our policy is that we set for that race, every car is checked on that list for that day. Crew chiefs have to put every template on every car that they bring to the racetrack, because they don't know which templates NASCAR is going to put on. And we always have the right, if we see something that doesn't look correct, to pull out another template."

Mechanical inspections are varied, too. One week, Nelson might decide that every set of rear-end gears must be completely torn down in inspection, but the next week it might be fuel cells or cylinder heads. As the theory goes, if the teams don't know what will be checked on a given weekend, the temptation to cheat is lessened—not eliminated, but at least lessened.

"Then we go through the prequalifying inspection, roll the car down under the close eye of all the officials, and actually escort the cars to pit road. Once they clear inspection, we don't lose sight of those cars until they get on the track and qualify," said Nelson. "When they come off the track, we'll take some random number of cars—maybe 10, maybe five—here at Daytona, we checked something on every car after qualifying. But at Rockingham, we'll pull out a number—

maybe the 19th qualifier and 12th qualifier or maybe 17th and 11th—we'll just pull numbers out, and those guys'll get checked. So nobody knows the random part of it, and the top two or three or five will always get checked after qualifying, engine, height, weight, and all that.

"We have a moving target when it comes to inspections. We don't think it's right to hide in the bushes and jump out and catch somebody. But we do feel it's important to be up front, check everybody the same, and let the guys know that there is not a pattern that they can draw from to understand or predict what they're going to get next."

After inspections are completed on race morning, the NASCAR workers officiate the race operation. "When they start the race our inspectors become officials. Now they're officiating pit stops, restarts, when to put out the yellow flag, when to put out the black flag, all the scoring and timing things that go on that officials do," said Nelson. "And when the race is over, they're back to being inspectors, and we're doing post-race inspections of competition items or safety investigations, too—people looking at cars that were wrecked."

A couple of times each year, NASCAR officials seize cars, usually the top-finishing or top two models of each brand, and take them to Lockheed's wind tunnel in Marietta, Georgia, for aerodynamic comparisons, to measure drag and downforce.

NASCAR also has a mobile chassis dyno, which it uses several times a year as part of post-race inspection to measure rear-wheel horsepower of competing cars, again typically taking six to eight of the top finishers. The thoroughness of today's inspection is due to several factors. NASCAR's desire to bring a new level of professionalism into the sport is the main one, but the phenomenal success of Jeff Gordon's team in the second half of the 1990s led other teams to put pressure on NASCAR to make sure Gordon's car was legal at all times. To prove to the other teams that Gordon wasn't cheating, NASCAR had to really tighten the screws in the inspection process.

"There was a lot of gray area before I got here," said Gordon's former crew chief Ray Evernham. "Gary Nelson will tell you I'm responsible for a lot of it being removed. I don't know if I should be proud of it or not. We never blatantly went out to cheat, but, boy, we worked hard in those gray areas. It's a fine line. When you're going to work in those gray areas, you've got to make sure that you know you're taking a chance to get slapped. When you get slapped, it's not nearly as funny as when you get around it. Gary reminded me there were 13 templates when I came to Winston Cup. Now I think there are 28 or 29. It's just a lot different. Inspection is a lot tighter, and the gray area is a lot smaller. The rule book has gotten a lot thicker chassis-wise and body-wise. It's not nearly as much fun as it used to be. You've got to read the rule book really, really hard to find the gray now."

And if one team finds too much gray area, it has the other teams to answer to.

"NASCAR uses the term 'their police department' to describe the competitors, 'cause most of them will see something before the inspectors do," said car owner Richard Childress. "That's how they learn about it. I've seen things get caught that you know NASCAR didn't catch until somebody came in and ratted them out. Our deal is if we see it's a gray area and you think you can get away with it, do it yourself until you get caught. As far as blatant cheating, cubic inches, a lot of things like that, tampering with your fuel, we just don't do it. We're watched so close, we're inspected so close by everybody in the garage area, plus NASCAR officials, that we can't do anything."

Few crew chiefs will admit that they've blown the whistle on fellow competitors. "I never did a lot of that," said McReynolds. "My theory was always if you saw something on another car, you needed to go back to work on your own car. I just didn't believe in running over to NASCAR and complaining, 'So-and-so's got this.' Now I'll say this: A lot of times it was kind of a relief when NASCAR would come up with a cut-and-dried rule over something that you knew was going to cover everybody. That could save you a lot of work and a lot of headache and a lot of heartache."

Still, admitted McReynolds, "NASCAR's best inspectors are all the competitors. They don't necessarily have to send inspectors out there."

"We watch," agreed Tommy Baldwin, crew chief for Ward Burton's Bill Davis Racing Dodge Intrepid R/T. "I think there's a common rule: We'll watch, but we won't throw each other in the river. We see what they're doing. We might go back to the shop and evaluate that during the week and see if it's a plus or a minus for us. We see things and we watch things. And the closer you're up in the garage towards the good cars, the more you see. That's because they're trying to advance. The officials pay a lot more attention to the lead cars, and you've got to be a lot more careful. You've got to be within their guidelines, and that's what we're trying to do."

Sometimes what crew chiefs watch are things like body contours; other times it's new equipment that shows up in the garage. During Evernham's tenure at Hendrick Motorsports, for example, he started using heaters to warm the bearings in the front axles of Jeff Gordon's Chevrolets before qualifying. In 2000, Todd Parrott was the first to hit on the idea of using a $50,000 electronic machine to measure the spring rate of each of Dale Jarrett's tires in an attempt to find more consistency. But such esoteric approaches only serve to reinforce the idea that today's rules limit the scope of "innovations" teams can hunt for.

"NASCAR pretty much came along a few years ago and hit on three distinct things that they're pretty adamant that they're not going to mess around with," said McReynolds. "That's big engines, playing with your tires and fuel. . . . If you get caught doing that, it could be 12 weeks' suspension for you, your driver, and/or your owner. And with the sponsors we got in this garage area, that's the last thing that you need. What terrible bad press for sponsorships, having those things come along. With the money that these people are spending, you don't need that kind of publicity."

Hand-in-hand with NASCAR's written law is an unspoken one in the garage: Crew chiefs understand that it's OK to try and circumvent the rule book up to a point. If you get caught with a car that fails inspection over an irregularity that legitimately can be chalked up to a difference of opinion in reading the rule book, that's OK. If you get caught flagrantly cheating, it can cost you big time.

"My former car owner Kenny Bernstein pretty much laid the law down for me," McReynolds said. "He said, 'I want you working as hard as you can, trying to get every advantage you can, but if you go too far off in the gray area, as long as I know about it, we'll be OK. But if I ever get a shock or a surprise, if you have done something that's going to cause us a lot of problems and I don't know about it, you're going to have a lot bigger problem on your hands.'"

At Daytona in 2001, there were plenty of examples of honest mistakes and one or two bigger problems. In fact, from the moment the NASCAR Winston Cup teams rolled through the gates of Daytona International Speedway, the battle of wits between NASCAR inspectors and team crew chiefs was at a fever pitch.

While the Winston Cup drivers spent February 8 in a mandatory "media day" event, schmoozing with journalists and getting their promo pictures taken in a huge tent outside the speedway, tech inspection inside the track was not going well. Just as at Talladega 10 months earlier, teams were trying to cheat the air with slicked-back bodywork, while inspectors were trying to detect every infraction.

And just as at Talladega, car owner Richard Childress was ordered to make substantial bodywork modifications on both of his team's Chevrolet Monte Carlos, which had been carefully prepared for drivers Dale Earnhardt and Mike Skinner. But while the Childress-NASCAR battle had taken center stage at Talladega, here its significance was dwarfed by the largest collection of unapproved parts and illegal cars anyone had seen in recent memory.

During practice February 9 and Daytona 500 pole qualifying February 10, Winston Cup Director Gary Nelson and his crew of inspectors seized so many illegal parts and fined so many crew chiefs that Nelson decided to hold an impromptu press conference late on the afternoon of February 12 to explain the specific penalties and his newly revised philosophy about how best to dispense justice in the Winston Cup garage.

There was much at stake for both NASCAR and the 55 teams entered at the race. The 2001 Daytona 500 was a landmark event for the sanctioning body: The race marked the return of Dodge to Winston Cup racing after an absence of more than two decades. It was also the first race broadcast by Rupert Murdoch's Fox television network, the kickoff event for a six-year, $2.4-billion television deal that firmly established NASCAR as one of the country's four major sports alongside Major League Baseball, the National Football League, and the National Basketball Association.

The Daytona weekend also marked the kickoff of the redesigned NASCAR Online Web site, another new and lucrative partnership for the sanctioning body, this one in conjunction with media giant AOL Time Warner and its Turner Interactive division.

The politics of it all, as always, were Byzantine. Though few would say so publicly, the team owners were furious that they weren't getting a bigger cut of the television money. And just a few weeks earlier, in an almost unprecedented show of unity, they banded together and rejected Turner's low-ball offer to buy up their individual team and driver Web sites.

But it was the return of Dodge that both created the greatest buzz and raised the most eyebrows. Dodge had invested tens of millions of dollars to return to Winston Cup, launching one of the most expensive advertising campaigns in history and lending unprecedented levels of technical support to its five-team, 10-car effort.

From one end of Daytona Beach to the other, there were Dodge posters at bus stops, huge murals hanging from hotels and the convention center, and a four-acre display where professional sports-car drivers took passengers around for hot laps in Dodge Vipers. The Adams Mark Hotel's credit-card-sized electronic room keys had pictures of all the Dodge cars imprinted on them.

For some competitors, the implication was simple: Given Dodge's massive investment in the sport, NASCAR would bend over backward to make sure the Dodges were competitive at Daytona. Rival Ford and General Motors team owners had quietly complained that NASCAR had given Dodge too much leeway in developing the bodywork and engine for its new Intrepid R/T Winston Cup car. And after being dog slow all during winter testing, all of a sudden the Dodges looked like the cars to beat at Daytona. Bill Elliott put Ray Evernham's Dodge Intrepid on the pole for the Daytona 500, with Stacy Compton qualifying second. Sterling Marlin won one of the Twin 125 qualifying races and all 10 of the Dodges made the race, prompting some pundits to claim the fix was in, that the game was tilted in Dodge's favor.

"Ray Charles could have seen this coming," said veteran motorsports journalist Mike Snow.

Nelson and the rest of the NASCAR officials were aware of the grumblings in the garage, which made it more important than ever to show that the sanctioning body wasn't discriminating for or against any one make of cars. So it came as no surprise that inspections were tighter than ever, especially since NASCAR had devoted much of the ever-shorter off-season to training inspectors on how to police the cars.

Although they publicly denied cracking down on the legality of cars at Daytona, inspectors found more infractions than usual. Some fell into the "gray areas" Nelson often talks about, while others were blatant and flagrant attempts to circumvent the rules.

So when Nelson walked into the Daytona infield media center shortly after 5 p.m. on February 12, he had no shortage of topics to talk about. "We started talking to people this morning about 9:30 and just finished about 15 minutes ago," Nelson said. "The interesting part is there's a story behind every one of these, and I heard 'em all today. It was a long day."

Heading the list of scofflaws with stories to tell was Tony Furr, crew chief for Jerry Nadeau's Hendrick Motorsports Chevrolet. Nadeau, an affable young driver, had blossomed in 2000 after struggling in his first two seasons.

Nadeau moved to the powerhouse Hendrick organization the previous season, winning his first Winston Cup race in the 2000 season finale at Atlanta. And Nadeau and Hendrick came to Daytona showcasing a lucrative new sponsorship deal with UAW and Delphi, who collectively ponied up roughly $10 million to sponsor the team for 2001.

When Nadeau appeared to qualify second for the Daytona 500, it didn't come as much of a shock to fans watching the race. But to his fellow competitors, it was another matter entirely. After Nadeau's qualifying run, several teams radioed NASCAR to say they saw something fall off the right rear of his car. The something was an illegal spacer inserted into the jack screw/spring plate assembly on the right rear of the car. The spacer had been cleverly engineered to hold the right rear of the car at legal height until it hit the first bump at speed. Then it would fall out, lowering the car and giving it less aero-dynamic drag, thereby increasing speed. Furr's device was not a "gray area" item, not something "pushing the envelope." It was a flagrant attempt to circumvent the rules, and it wasn't the only such infraction that would be found on the car that weekend.

"The cleanup crew found one of the parts on the racetrack," Nelson said of the suspension components on Nadeau's car. "This piece was designed to break away or fall out when the car was on the racetrack. So when the inspector looked at it, it looked like a normal piece, but when the car got on the race-track, it popped out and the car got that much lower." It wasn't much more sophisticated than the rocks and sticks mechan-ics from the 1960s used to jam in the springs at Daytona to keep the cars up during inspection, only to fall out once the car hit the first bump at speed.

During post-qualifying inspection, NASCAR varies what it checks on each car. According to Nelson, somewhere between eight and 15 cars went through minimum height inspection after Daytona 500 qualifying, and here Nadeau's car came up half an inch too low. With 55 cars entered, Furr evidently thought the odds of getting checked were worth the risk of a penalty. He was wrong, and Nelson was not amused.

"We went to the crew and said, 'What were you thinking?'" Nelson said. "And we did not get an answer." What they did get, though, were more infractions. Nadeau's car was found to have an illegal fuel cell made of too-thin metal. According to Nelson, this infraction was every bit as flagrant as the rear suspension spacer was: The fuel cell was the proper thickness of metal where NASCAR usually measures it, but too thin everywhere else. Crew chiefs have been known to use compressed air to expand a "thin-wall" fuel tank just enough to fit another gallon of gas in it, which can make the difference between winning or losing, especially at a place like Daytona.

As a result of his actions, Furr earned $12,750 in fines and a four-race suspension. Nadeau's qualifying time was disallowed as well. "When you look at Tony Furr's car this weekend, you've got a car that was too low after qualifying, a part designed to break the rules, to take away positions from other competitors in the garage who did it right," said Nelson. "And we had [an illegal] fuel cell on the 25 car. Tony Furr has done a lot just this weekend. Just on that alone, if you took a survey of crew chiefs and asked them what do you think about a guy who got caught with these things this weekend, I think they would agree that a suspension is the proper thing to do."

"We made a mistake and we're paying for it, simple as that. That's all I can say," Furr said, when asked about the rules infractions. "Hopefully, it'll send a message out to make everybody quit. This may make everything a little more equal." This from the same crew chief who got caught in practice at the same track in July 1997 with illegal carburetor studs on John Andretti's car, a car which would go on to win that race.

Of course, Furr was far from the only offender at Daytona this time. On February 12, NASCAR announced that Jason Leffler's Chip Ganassi Racing Dodge Intrepid R/T had been caught with a "discrepancy" in its fuel supply. Leffler's Daytona 500 qualifying time was disallowed, as Nadeau's had been. His crew chief, Kevin Cram, also was suspended for four races and received a $10,000 fine. Both Cram's and Furr's suspensions would begin February 23 at North Carolina Speedway.

Just like Jeremy Mayfield's tainted fuel controversy at Talladega in 2000, Leffler's crew professed not to know how it happened. "Even though this news comes as a surprise to all of us, we are looking into the matter and will abide by NASCAR's ruling," Ganassi Team Manager Andy Graves said.

Felix Sabates, the team's former owner and now a minority partner to Ganassi, suspected sabotage, but offered little explanation as to motivation or how the sabotage may have happened—the exact strategy employed by Mayfield's car owner, Michael Kranefuss, after that team's incident.

"I really believe somebody actively sabotaged the car," Sabates said. "There's no doubt in my mind. The other guys on the team don't want to say anything because they have to live with these people every weekend [but] I believe it in my heart that they did."

Ultimately, the team would pay a huge price for their transgression. By midseason, first-year sponsor Cingular Wireless had notified the team that it would not be back for the 2002 season. Instead, it moved to Richard Childress Racing.

NASCAR inspectors were busy elsewhere, too. They seized oversized fuel cells from cars driven by Dale Earnhardt, Jeff Burton, Joe Nemechek, Kenny Wallace, and Steve Park. Nemechek also had his windshield taken because it didn't fit NASCAR templates. Front suspension A-arms that didn't meet minimum thicknesses were confiscated from the cars of Bill Elliott and Andy Houston, and Terry Labonte's Chevrolet had both a roof spoiler and body filler material taken.

Four cars—those driven by Jeff Gordon, Todd Bodine, Steve Park, and Morgan Shepherd—had fuel cell intake caps seized for various modifications. Gordon also was nabbed with an unapproved air deflector, and Mike Skinner's car had an underpan removed.

Unapproved rear springs that failed to meet NASCAR's mandated minimum of 345 pounds of resistance were taken from the cars of second-qualifier Stacy Compton, Dale Jarrett, Casey Atwood, Morgan Shepherd, and Norm Benning.

But the hottest items NASCAR inspectors found were adjustable—and therefore, illegal—body braces, which could be used to pull the sheet metal in closer to create just a little less aerodynamic drag. Those nabbed with these parts included Bodine, Nadeau, Leffler, Mike Wallace, Ricky Craven, Rusty Wallace, and Casey Atwood. The devices were similar to the turnbuckles used by some of the Ford teams at Daytona nearly 40 years earlier, when teams were just starting to figure out that the way you went faster was to lessen aero-dynamic drag.

The Richard Childress Racing Chevrolet Monte Carlos of Earnhardt and Skinner were forced to make extensive body-work modifications to pass tech inspections. By the end of the weekend, 18 crew chiefs had been fined and two suspended, in a crackdown unlike any other in recent memory. Hendrick Motorsports had the dubious honor of having all three of its crew chiefs on the receiving end of Nelson's penalties: Furr was suspended; Gary DeHart was put on probation for infractions found on Terry Labonte's car; and Robbie Loomis was fined for work done on Jeff Gordon's car.

The way Nelson dispensed his brand of justice at Daytona also marked a major philosophical change for NASCAR. In the mid-1990s, the sanctioning body tried ever-increasing fines to punish crew chiefs. But starting with the 2001 Daytona 500, Nelson said the sanctioning body would begin relying more on suspensions and putting together "rap sheets" to be used in the future against repeat offenders.

"As we started raising these fines, we started looking around and seeing that the sponsorship dollars, the purse dollars, the money was going up so much that the fines really weren't getting the message across," Nelson explained. "We were still finding things. It might have worked for maybe six months or a year where we went pretty clean for a while, but now, last year and this year, things started coming up again. The message to the teams is, it's a good way to get suspended if you break one of these major rules. . . . Also now we started to build a case or a file on that individual.

"A lot of times we'd be in conversations with crew chiefs and they'd say, 'Look, I've never done anything,'" Nelson continued. "'What are you doing with me?' In my memory, I go, 'Look, back at Daytona I took some parts from you, didn't I?' 'No, that wasn't me, that was so-and-so.' Now, we got a file for everything we take that has any significance at all. That is part of that individual's record that will follow him through any future problems that we may have."

Part of Nelson's challenge is similar to that of any judge: He has to interpret both the rules and the motivation of those who break them. For example, Loomis was caught at Daytona with an unapproved air deflector underneath the front of three-time champion Gordon's No. 24 Hendrick Motorsports Chevrolet. He got off with a modest fine and no suspension, while fellow Hendrick crew chief DeHart was put on probation for improperly mounting the roof spoiler on Terry Labonte's car.

"The entry blank for the Daytona 500 and the Bud Shootout had a full paragraph describing how to put the roof deflector on the car, where to fit it, how it's to be mounted, what you can and cannot do about it," Nelson said. "There was no gray area on how that deflector was to be mounted. Every team got that entry blank, read it. Most of 'em called me and asked me questions about it. The difference in what Robbie did was, yeah, that's a gray area in the rule book. It would have probably gone without a penalty except for the fact that he made it out of clear plastic in hopes that we would not see it and take it from him. So he was hoping we'd roll under the car and see through it and not notice it. He said, 'I knew it probably wasn't legal, but I figured if I make it clear you might not see it and I might get away with it.'"

And yet, through all the controversy and the stash of confiscated parts, most competitors held their ground about their actions.

Ray Evernham, car owner for the Daytona 500 pole-winning Dodge of Bill Elliott and also Casey Atwood's, made no apologies about the fact that his two cars needed a little tweaking to pass inspection. "I know we had to do some work on both cars, not a lot," Evernham said. "You're trying to hold tolerances of .060 of an inch and get any advantage you can, and I would have been a little disappointed if they didn't have to work on any one of those cars."

"A lot of these guys will come and they'll make big changes and stretch the rules a little further than they need to be. You try and find that limit and stay there. We really didn't have to make any large changes, but when we unloaded we were fairly close," added Mike Ford, Elliott's crew chief. "You try and take everything you can, because you do have tolerances. Like Ray mentioned, you try to stick within 0.060s. It's the guy who can stick within 0.020s that ends up being the guy to beat. We tried to step it to 0.010s. We worked extra hard to make sure we took everything that we could get and try and not go over the line."

And Mike Ford made no bones about the fact that the limit gets stretched most often for the Daytona 500. "If you look at it, it's the biggest race of the year, you have the most time to prepare," he said. "It's bragging rights, more or less. It's the big race, the one everybody wants to win. You definitely want to qualify well. It's a big push to try and come down here and do well," he said.

Compton, who like many drivers, made several trips through tech before his car was cleared for inspection, was philosophical about the process. "Everything you do, you do it on the limit," he said. "Everything we do, everything that Ray [Evernham] does, everything that [Robert] Yates does, everything is right on the edge. You push it as far as you possibly can. We have a lot of things that are right on the edge, but 99.9 percent of 'em got through.

"You know when you come down here that you're not going to get through tech the first time. I don't think there's a single car that did," he continued. "And we were actually pleased that we got through. We made two small changes the first time we went through and NASCAR said everything's great. We got our sticker and went out practicing."

To Compton, this was all no big deal. "That's all part of the game," he said, "As Gary Nelson says, there's 600 of you guys (crewmen) trying to outsmart 30 of us [inspectors]. Everybody is doing what I said. [NASCAR requires] a 345-pound rear spring in the rear, we try and go through with a 344-pound spring. You've got to take that chance. You've got to try and get everything you can get. That's the reason I saw about 20 springs sitting out there that had failed [inspection]. When I came through Thursday evening, there was a whole lot of sheet metal being removed and replaced and a whole lot of grinding going on."

Still there are limits. "You just can't do stupid things like that and expect to get away with it," said Tommy Baldwin.

"NASCAR's pretty on top of those things. You know, a lot of those piles of parts on that table, a lot of them are honest mistakes. Some of 'em aren't. You try to get away with what you can, but you've got a lot riding nowadays. You've got major corporations spending millions of dollars and car owners that are spending millions of dollars. You can't get that reputation [as a cheater], and I think some people in the garage have a reputation of doing that, and I think it's going to be tough getting jobs in the future."

But cheating is tempting, if for no other reason than the odds remain in favor of the teams, not NASCAR. "It's impossible to catch everything," said 1980 Daytona 500 champion Buddy Baker. "There's still some people laughing that they got caught and making comments about somebody else getting in trouble, and they're probably sitting there with about the same stuff and just hasn't been caught yet. Boy, I'll tell you, back home it doesn't look so bad when you're 'fixing' it," he laughed when describing some of the creative preparations on the various race cars. "You get down here and you get caught, it looks awful."

• • •

Nelson is nearly mobbed at his press conference, with the usual assortment of motorsports journalists being joined by maybe 100 more reporters eager to see the first race of NASCAR's new television and Internet partnerships and Dodge's return.

Toward the end of the press conference, Nelson is asked point blank if NASCAR competitors are simply a bunch of cheaters. "What we have is what we have," he shrugged. "We're not trying to gloss over anything. We've got individuals that violated our rules, and we are addressing it. From a sanctioning body, from an inspector, a NASCAR official's standpoint, we have to look at it like the best way to quit finding illegal parts is to convince 'em not to do it."

Later that week, Nelson would compare the spate of infractions in the garage to those in the world at large. "Racing is hard and there's always temptations, just like there's temptations in real life to break laws," Nelson said February 17. "But you try to understand that the majority of our garage follows the rules. There's only a few guys that try and take the shortcut and flat-out cheat. Life's the same way. If a convenience store has hundreds and thousands of customers, every once in a while, somebody tries to rob it. That's just a fact of life, and we deal with it in a way that we think discourages that kind of activity."

Sterling Marlin's Dodge Intrepid R/T rolls through the inspection area at Indianapolis in 2002. The competitors refer to the NASCAR Winston Cup garage inspection facility as the "room of doom." (Sam Sharpe)

Epilogue

When I got involved 13 years ago, there was a lot more cheating going on. Everybody broke the rules. They didn't bend them, they broke them.

—Felix Sabates

Epilogue
Sinning Anew

At Daytona in 2002, Jerry Nadeau's car flunked inspection after one of the Twin 125 qualifying races because it was too low. Hendrick Motorsports subsequently issued a statement from crew chief Tony Furr saying it was the result of a faulty spring that collapsed during the race "and was obviously in no way intentional, since such a defect can have a negative impact on the handling."

Readers will recall that Furr got caught at Daytona in 2001 with a car that was too low and a fuel cell that did not meet specs, and had been busted at Daytona in 1997 at Daytona for sliding carburetor studs.

The winner of the 2002 Daytona 500 was likable Ward Burton, his team run by Tommy Baldwin, a man who has strong opinions about a crew chief's responsibilities. At a panel discussion with NASCAR President Mike Helton and four other NASCAR experts in January 2000, Baldwin put it about as bluntly as one could. "If I can find a way to get an extra gallon of gas in my car, I'm going to win," he said.

Burton's 2002 Daytona victory came about because race leader Sterling Marlin got caught breaking the rules. While the race was stopped under a late red flag, Marlin hopped out of his car to pull a fender away from a tire, a clear violation that got him sent to the back of the field and put second-place runner Burton up front for good.

A week after Daytona, Matt Kenseth broke a nearly two-year non-winning streak with a win at Rockingham in his Jack Roush–owned Ford. His car failed post-race inspection because it was too low, and his team was fined $30,000 as a result. "I am sure that policing the race cars after the race each week is not one of the things that NASCAR relishes doing," Roush said after the race. "We believed that the 17 car [Kenseth's] was legal; we were surprised by the whole thing. We race each week for that last 1/16 of an inch in all areas, and if we set up our cars to have some comfort level in those areas then we can't be competitive. We have left it to NASCAR to exact the penalty, and we will not appeal it. We've appealed to NASCAR two other times when I have been quite sure that what we got was unwarranted, unsuccessfully, but I'm glad that NASCAR is taking care of business and I hope that we won't get caught out again."

Unbelievably, a week later at Las Vegas came more controversy. This time Marlin was caught speeding down the pit road during a pit stop, a violation that should have carried a 15-second penalty and dropped him to the very end of the field. But because of a radio communications snafu among NASCAR officials, the penalty was not communicated to Marlin's team until after his car left the pits. NASCAR decided it would be unfair to bring him back into the pits, and the penalty was never enforced. Marlin went on to win the race.

In other words, the game continues, exactly as it has from the very beginning, from the days when Glenn Dunnaway and Big Bill France were embroiled in controversy and the court system in 1949, on through Smokey Yunick, Junior Johnson, and Gary Nelson. If you look at the sport of stock-car racing today versus its infancy more than half a century ago, everything is different, yet in some respects nothing's changed. The name of the game is still beating the other guy, either by out-driving him or simply by building a faster, better race car.

The four years I was fortunate enough to spend making my living in racing afforded me some up-close insights into the process that few fans, even the most ardent ones, would ever have the opportunity to experience.

By whatever name you choose to call it or whatever phraseology you use, cheating in one form or another has always been a part of the sport of stock-car racing. It affected the outcome of the first NASCAR Strictly Stock race on a dusty dirt track in Charlotte, North Carolina, in 1949, and it was the biggest pre-race story at the 2001 Daytona 500. And one way or another, it's been there in all the years in between.

Men who race hate the word "cheat," yet it hasn't stopped many of them from doing it. It's easy to understand why: They either want to win or run well enough to keep their jobs and their sponsors.

And while in the cold, clear light of day, it's easy for me or anyone else who is not a Winston Cup competitor to look upon some of the things that have happened and say they were wrong, the morality is a little more complicated for those in the sport. Ultimately, it's up to each reader to draw his or her own conclusions about how they feel about cheating; who did what, and when; and whether or not those actions diminish the accomplishments and records of the men who committed them.

But after this two-year odyssey of research into the subject, I am convinced of only two things: One, racers will never stop looking for ways to circumvent the rules and are doing it even as you are reading this. Two, for its many faults, NASCAR is doing a better job than ever of trying to level the playing field and keep the sport fair for all concerned.

Gary Nelson, who took over as Winston Cup director in 1992 and was promoted to NASCAR managing director of competition for 2002, has drawn both praise and a tremendous amount of heat from competitors, media, and fans alike. If Fords win too many races, then the GM and Dodge teams complain bitterly and publicly. If Jeff Gordon wins, fans think it's because NASCAR has rigged the races. If a race ends under caution, fans want to know why it wasn't red-flagged so that it can end under green and vice-versa.

But despite the frequent criticism, I truly believe Nelson has done everything within his power to make the sport as fair as he possibly can. You don't see guys running tires filled with water anymore, or roll cages with fuel lines running through them or 7/8-scale bodies get through inspection.

"When I got involved 13 years ago, there was a lot more cheating going on," Felix Sabates told me before the 2001 Daytona 500. "Everybody broke the rules. They didn't bend them, they broke them. I think it's a lot fairer today. I think the competition is more fair. I think they [NASCAR] are more fair with the teams. I think they're looking at teams as their business partners now rather than the enemy."

"They do inspections out in the open now. You don't have to take anybody's word for it," added Robert Yates. "You can observe. That's probably why there are so many cars running within a foot of each other. A lot of that you have to attribute to the fairness of the rules and keeping everybody straight. That's a good thing. We don't get upset by having to take their word that somebody is right. We pretty much get to be shown. If our vision is good, we can see for ourselves. That's taken so much of the cheating deal out of it."

Of course, that doesn't mean people have quit trying to be creative. "We're going to try to slip it by them, and if we can slip one by, more power to us," laughed Sabates, when asked if teams still look for an edge.

Just like they always have and always will.

CHEATING

Index

A

AAA division, 51, 150
Adams Mark Hotel, 224
Aerodynamics
 aluminum fenders and, 80-81
 auto roofs and, 78
 body braces and, 229
 downforce and, 129-130
 horsepower and, 66, 81
 Junior Johnson on, 40
 low-speed tracks and, 192
 nose lowering and, 78-79, 90-95,
  102-103, 135
 painting and, 103-104
 templates and, 66, 75, 95, 96, 129,
  130, 192, 216
 wind resistance and, 77
 Yunick and, 61-62, 66, 71
Air deflectors, 114, 229, 231
Allison, Bobby, 107, 109, 110, 123,
 126-127
Allison, Carl, 32
Allison, David, 32
Allison, Donnie, 113
Aluminum fenders, 80-81
American Racing Classics, 57
Andretti, John, 166-167, 228
Andretti, Mario, 97
Andy Petree Racing, 131
Anheuser-Busch, 150
AOL Time Warner, 223
ARCA series, 204
Atlanta Motor Speedway, 10, 27, 92,
 173
Atwood, Casey, 229, 232
Automobiles. *See* specific
 manufacturers
Auton, Wayne, 184
Axles, cambered rear axles, 16

B

Baker, Buck, 33, 51
Baker, Buddy, 153
Baker, "Cannonball," 29, 50
Baldwin, Tommy, 220-221, 233-
 234, 238
Beam, Mike, 156
Beaty, Dick
 inspections and, 141
 lead-weight cheating and, 87
 Gary Nelson and, 151
 retirement of, 153

roller-tappet cheating and,
 110-111
Roush Racing and, 147
as Winston Cup director, 127
Yunick and, 59-60
Bellhousings, 61
Benning, Norm, 229
Benson, Johnny, 198
Bernstein, Kenny, 222
Bettenhausen, Tony, 51
Bickford, John, 156, 172, 174, 180-
 182, 183, 186
Bickle, Rich, 168
Biffle, Greg, 184, 186, 196
Bill Davis Racing, 220
Bodine, Brett, 168
Bodine, Geoff, 149, 151
Bodine, Todd, 229
Body braces, 229
Bondo, 193
"Bootlegger springs," 11, 33
Bore, 125, 149
Brewer, Tim, 149-151
Brickyard 400, 115
Bristol Motor Speedway, 176, 192
Bud Shootout, 231
Budweiser, 18, 150
Buicks, 33, 50, 126
Bull, David, 10
Bureau of Alcohol, Tobacco and
 Firearms, 30
Burton, Jeff, 164, 175, 229
Burton, Ward, 175, 220, 238-239
Busch beer, 150
Busch Series, 196-198
Byron, Red, 37-38, 46, 53

C

C pillars, 192
C post templates, 130
Cadillac, 31, 38
California Speedway, 197
Cambered rear axles, 16
Carburetors
 carburetor plates, 107
 carburetor spacers, 145, 147-148
 carburetor studs, 166, 228, 238
 insert modifications for, 167
 inspections and, 75, 194
 Stromberg carburetors, 41
CART FedEx Championship Series,
 206
Cavin, Curt, 115, 116
Champ cars, 14
Charlotte Motor Speedway
 disqualifications at, 107

first stock-car race and, 26
Gordon and, 158
inspections at, 110
National 500, 106-107
public relations directors, 27
race weight and, 105
scandals involving, 120-127
Strictly Stock race, 32
Charlotte Observer, 35, 75, 94, 171,
 203
Charlotte/Douglas International
 Airport, 127
Chassis, 74
Cheating. *See also* Fines; Fuel;
 Intake manifold; and specific
 auto parts, drivers, and races
 acknowledgement of, 11-13
 "cheat neat" philosophy, 76, 132
 competitive edge and, 14-15
 costs of, 50
 fenders and, 80-81
 justification for, 14, 53
 mistakes and, 145, 234
 nose lowering and, 78-80, 90-95,
  102-103
 on race weight, 16, 20, 86-88, 101-
  102, 106, 152, 181-182
 prevalence of, 10-11, 219-220
 publicity and, 221
 restrictor plates and, 111-113, 190
 scalloping as, 166
 secrecy and, 81-82, 104-105
 shocks and, 90-91
 suspensions and, 150-151, 199,
  227, 228, 230
 temptation for, 18, 234
 tire-related cheating, 11, 103, 178
Chevrolet
 Camaros, 85
 Chevelles, 71, 93, 94
 Childress and, 191
 Daytona 500 and, 151
 Earnhardt and, 193
 economy cars and, 100
 Evernham and, 221
 Glotzbach and, 107
 Hendrick Motorsports and, 173,
  209
 inspections and, 132
 Junior Johnson and, 120
 Marlin and, 194
 McLaren-Mercedes Formula One
  team and, 206
 modifications on, 152
 Monte Carlo, 113, 169-171, 222,
  230
 Thomas and, 39
 Vega, 100